T0155200

ADVANCING STUDENT ACHIEVEMENT

EDUCATION
next
B O O K S

The Hoover Institution and Education Next Books
gratefully acknowledge the following individuals
and foundations for their support of this research on
education policy and reform.

LYNDE AND HARRY BRADLEY FOUNDATION

KORET FOUNDATION

EDMUND AND JEANNIK LITTLEFIELD FOUNDATION

BERNARD AND CATHERINE SCHWARTZ FOUNDATION

WILLIAM E. SIMON FOUNDATION

BOYD AND JILL SMITH

TAD AND DIANNE TAUBE FOUNDATION

JACK AND MARY WHEATLEY

THE HOOVER INSTITUTION'S KORET TASK FORCE ON K–12 EDUCATION

ADVANCING STUDENT ACHIEVEMENT

Herbert J. Walberg

HOOVER INSTITUTION PRESS

STANFORD UNIVERSITY

STANFORD, CALIFORNIA

The Hoover Institution on War, Revolution and Peace, founded at Stanford University in 1919 by Herbert Hoover, who went on to become the thirty-first president of the United States, is an interdisciplinary research center for advanced study on domestic and international affairs. The views expressed in its publications are entirely those of the authors and do not necessarily reflect the views of the staff, officers, or Board of Overseers of the Hoover Institution.

www.hoover.org

EDUCATION next
B O O K S

An imprint of the Hoover Institution Press
Hoover Institution Press Publication No. 568
Copyright © 2010 by the Board of Trustees of the Leland Stanford Junior University

All rights reserved. No part of this publication may be reproduced, stored in a retrieval system, or transmitted in any form or by any means, electronic, mechanical, photocopying, recording, or otherwise, without written permission of the publisher.

First printing, 2010
17 16 15 14 13 12 11 10   9 8 7 6 5 4 3 2 1

Manufactured in the United States of America

The paper used in this publication meets the minimum requirements of the American National Standard for Information Sciences—Permanence of Paper for Printed Library Materials, ANSI Z39.48–1992.

Library of Congress Cataloging-in-Publication Data
  Walberg, Herbert J., 1937–
  Advancing student achievement / by Herbert J. Walberg.
     p.   cm.— (Hoover Institution Press publication series ; No. 568)
  Includes bibliographical references and index.
  ISBN-13: 978-0-8179-4951-8 (hardback : alk. paper)
  ISBN-13: 978-0-8179-4952-5 (pbk. : alk. paper)
  ISBN-13: 978-0-8179-4953-2 (e-book)
  1. School improvement programs—United States.   2. Academic achievement—United States.   3. Educational psychology—United States.   I. Title.
LB2822.82.W35   2010
371.2′070973—dc22   2008052478

CONTENTS

PREFACE

My purposes in writing this book were to describe how students learn, and to explain how family, classroom, and school practices can help them learn more. I also wanted to describe the research methods and evidence for the findings and to refer readers to further research and practical information.

This book derives primarily from behavioral psychology, which emphasizes objective observation and measurement of desired behaviors (or outcomes), and how changes in organization, policies, and practices affect them. The research described here explores how teachers, parents, and others affect student learning. As the term implies, behavioral research usually puts little emphasis on self-reports about internal states such as self-esteem because they cannot be objectively measured or observed.

The evidence in this book is largely restricted to studies of learning outcomes, particularly achievement tests. When well designed and constructed, such tests are objective and reliable. As documented in subsequent chapters, citizens, legislators, parents, and students themselves widely support achievement measurement.

A secondary source of evidence in this book is economics, which shares with behavioral psychology the study of observable and measurable causes and desirable effects. Economists working in K–12 education have often defined learning as the desired effect, making their findings relevant to my purposes.

Economic research that challenges assumptions about causal

effects can be particularly valuable. As described in this book, for example, economists' studies of teacher credentials indicate that education and experience have surprisingly little or no effect on student learning. This negative finding is useful because it suggests that the usual teacher credentialing and compensation show little promise to improve learning. Economists have also carried out rigorous studies of school choice that suggest that consumer choice works well in schools, as it does in markets and other social enterprises. Because of such insights from economists, I have freely drawn on their research as well as that in my own field of psychology.

HERBERT J. WALBERG
Chicago, Illinois
January 2010

ACKNOWLEDGMENTS

My present academic appointment at Stanford University's Hoover Institution enables me, as a member of the Koret Task Force on K–12 Education, to meet twice a year with its distinguished members—John Chubb, Williamson Evers, Chester Finn, Eric Hanushek, Paul Hill, E.D. Hirsch, Caroline Hoxby, Tom Loveless, Terry Moe, and Paul Peterson. I am grateful to them for their oral and written comments on previous versions of this book and to Hoover Director John Raisian and Associate Director Richard Sousa for their encouragement and support.

Sponsored by the U.S. Department of Education, the National Center on School Choice at Vanderbilt University stimulated my thinking and writing. My work there, including that on the *Handbook of Research on School Choice,* co-edited with the center's Director Mark Berends and colleagues Dale Ballou and Matthew Springer, informed and motivated me in writing the present book.

For me, it is an honor to be a trustee of the Foundation for Teaching Economics, which provides scholarships for high school teachers and students to study economics. Until his death, Milton Friedman, perhaps the most important school-choice leader of modern times, advised the foundation. Its present board has two Nobel laureates, Douglass North and Vernon Smith, as well as board chairman William Hume, President Gary Walton, and other leading academic and business leaders.

A special thanks goes to Joe Bast, president of the Heartland Institute, whose board I chair. In writing two previous books with him and collaborating on many projects, I learned much about economics and policy.

Finally, I thank people who carefully reviewed and made suggestions on previous parts or the whole of this book—Marshall Blanshard, Anders Ericsson, Robin Fern, Steven Graubart, Manisha Singh, Winnie Stariha, John Stone, Adam Tanney, Trudy Wallace, and Genevieve Zottola. Needless to say, the opinions expressed and any remaining errors are attributable only to me.

HERBERT J. WALBERG
Chicago, Illinois
January 2010

1

INTRODUCTION

A 1983 report to the U.S. Secretary of Education, *A Nation at Risk*, drew attention to the poor mathematics and science achievement of American students relative to those in other economically advanced countries.[1] A 1998 report, *A Nation Still at Risk*, pointed out how little progress had been made.[2]

A response to these risks, the report *Goals 2000*, for better or worse, recommended centralizing the nation's school system in an effort to raise standards and measure achievement on a national level.[3] Additional research, reports, conventions, and policies spun out of *A Nation at Risk* and culminated in the 2002 federal legislation known as No Child Left Behind, which in principle required schools to meet new standards as indicated by achievement test performance.[4]

For the last half-century, however, higher spending and many

---

1. U.S. Department of Education, *A Nation at Risk* (Washington, DC, 1983).

2. William J. Bennett, Willard Fair, Chester E. Finn, Floyd H. Flake, E.D. Hirsch, Will Marshall, and Diane Ravitch, "A Nation Still at Risk," *Policy Review* 90, (1988): 23–29.

3. William J. Jeynes, *American Educational History: School, Society, and the Common Good* (Thousand Oaks, CA: Sage Publications, 2007).

4. Patrick J. McGuinn, *No Child Left Behind: and the Transformation of Federal Education Policy, 1965–2005* (Lawrence, KS: Lawrence University Press of Kansas, 2006).

reforms failed to raise achievement to the high levels of other economically advanced countries.[5] A recent international achievement study showed, for example, that among students in 30 countries, those in the United States ranked 25th in science, exceeding only Portugal, Italy, Greece, Turkey, and Mexico.

American students also do poorly in language. The 2008 report of the National Assessment of Educational Progress (NAEP), for example, showed that only an estimated 24 percent of 12th graders showed proficiency in writing as indicated by correct spelling, appropriate grammar, and the skills needed to write an essay and explain complex information.[6] Only 31 percent of 8th graders showed adequate reading skills. Language skills, particularly reading, are essential for further learning in school subjects and have important economic and social significance.

John Bormuth's unique reading survey of about 5,000 people aged 16 and over showed that 87 percent of those employed reported that they had to read as part of their jobs.[7] Typical workers read 141 minutes per day as part of their jobs, or about 29 percent of the workday. Since the national wage bill in 1971 was $859 billion, Bormuth estimated that U.S. workers earned $253 billion for on-the-job reading. Since there are more workers today who undoubtedly read even more at higher hourly wages, the amount paid for on-the-job reading must be substantially greater.

Arguably, U.S. workers receive more pay for reading than any other activity. Yet, American youth are ill prepared in reading as

---

5. Caroline M. Hoxby, "Are Efficiency and Equity in School Finance Substitutes or Complements?" *Journal of Economic Perspectives,* 10(4), (2007): 51–72. See also Organization for Economic Co-operation and Development, Program for International Student Assessment (PISA), 2006: *Science Competencies for Tomorrow's World* (Paris: December 2007).

6. Deborah Salahu-Din, Hillary Persky, and Jessica Miller, *The Nation's Report Card: Writing 2007* (NCES 2008–468). (Washington, DC: National Center for Education Statistics, Institute of Education Sciences, U.S. Department of Education, 2008).

7. John R. Bormuth, "Value and Volume of Literacy," *Visible Language* 12 (1978): 118–161.

well as mathematics and science for further education and work. Colleges and firms must provide costly remedial training to try to make up for prior years of lagging achievement.

DROPOUTS

The learning problem is also reflected in dropout rates. After World War II, the United States was notable for having comparatively large percentages of students entering and graduating from high school. But other countries have made rapid progress, and the United States now ranks poorly among other economically advanced countries. Between 1995 and 2005, for example, U.S. high school completion rates dropped from 2nd to 21st among 27 economically advanced countries even though U.S. per-student spending on schools was rising and had been (and still is) among the highest per-student school spenders of all economically advanced nations.

Only about 70 percent of American students graduate on time with a regular high school diploma and about 1.2 million students drop out annually. Seventeen of the nation's 50 largest cities have dropout rates greater than 50 percent.[8]

Poor achievement and less education deny young people prosperous, healthy lives. Adults with more education not only earn more but also live longer, save a larger fraction of their incomes, and invest more in their children. As noted by Gary Becker and Kevin Murphy in 2008, highly educated people excel in many aspects of life. "The education process itself leads people away from more harmful activities and toward better habits."[9]

Americans are deservedly concerned about the poor performance of K–12 students and the possible consequences for their

8. Christopher B. Swanson, *Cities in Crisis* (Washington, DC: America's Promise Alliance, 2008), http://www.americaspromise.org/APA.aspx.

9. Gary S. Becker and Kevin M. Murphy, "Inequality and Opportunity," *Capital Ideas* (May 2007): 4–7.

future and the nation's. As a result of inferior achievement, the United States grew at a lower rate than its potential,[10] reducing the quality of life at least insofar as purchasing power is concerned. For 2007 alone, the loss was an estimated $300 billion. Because we live in an information age of increasing global competition, knowledge and skill deficits could be far more damaging in the future. One consequence is growing job outsourcing to other countries, not only in manufacturing but increasingly in services such as radiological diagnosis and software development.

THE PUBLIC'S SCHOOL REFORM VIEWS

The public appears to understand the learning problem and has astonishingly strong views about what to do about it. They favor much more accountability for schools, educators, and students. Many think students in repeatedly failing schools should be allowed to transfer elsewhere, and many see a need for replacing the faculty or closing such schools altogether.[11]

Only 11 percent of the public is against renewing federal legislation that requires states to set standards in mathematics and reading (or English language arts). They favor testing students each year to determine whether the standards are being met. More than 8 in 10 favor a policy of requiring students to pass an examination before they are eligible to move on to the next grade, and 85 percent support requiring a high school graduation examination.

Sixty percent of the surveyed public favors the publication of

---

10. Erik A. Hanushek and Ludvig Woessmann, *Education Quality and Economic Growth* (Washington, DC: World Bank, 2007).

11. William G. Howell, Martin R. West, and Paul E. Peterson, "What Americans Think about Their Schools." *Education Next* (fall 2007): 12–26. Though the public appears correct in their view that the schools are failing and that radical changes are called for, they may be naïve or rationalizing in saying that the schools their children attend are acceptable, a view similar to that in Lake Woebegone where it is joked that all the children are above average.

the average test scores of students in each public school. A similar percentage says that schools that fail to meet state standards for five consecutive years should be substantially reformed or closed, and only 4 percent of the public completely oppose teacher replacement; 3 percent completely oppose replacing the principal, and 14 percent completely oppose turning the school into a charter school. Only about one-fifth of the public completely oppose the use of government funds to pay the tuition of low-income students who choose to attend private schools.

Less than a third of the public opposes basing teacher salaries in part on students' academic progress on state tests. Sizable percentages of the population believe that teachers in challenging schools should get larger salaries, and that qualified teachers of mathematics and science, which are hard to recruit, should be given extra compensation.

Thus, the public favors both stricter enforcement of the present legislation as well as more radical reforms. Four decades after it became clear that U.S. students were falling behind those in other countries, and a quarter-century after publication of *A Nation at Risk*, citizens have come to hold radical views in contrast to those of the twentieth century.

STUDENTS' VERSUS EDUCATORS' VIEWS

Like the public, students—the direct clients of public schools—think their schools have been lax and should raise their standards. A Public Agenda national survey of high school students, for example, showed that three-fourths believe stiffer examinations and graduation requirements would make students pay more attention to their studies. Three-fourths said schools should promote only students who master the material. Almost two-thirds reported they could do much better in school if they tried. Nearly 80 percent said students would learn more if schools made sure they were on time and did their homework. More than 70 percent said schools should require after-school classes for those earning Ds and Fs.[12]

In these respects, educators on average differ sharply from students and the previously described views of the public. Interviews with a national representative sample of elementary- and secondary-school educators and students revealed the following percentages agreeing with the degree of academic challenge in their schools:[13]

View/Percentage Agreement	Principals	Teachers	Students
The school has high academic standards	71	60	38
The classes are challenging	67	48	23
The teachers have high expectations of students	56	39	25

The apparent slack standards of many practicing educators may derive from views prevalent in the schools of education they attended. A national survey[14] of education professors showed that only 12 percent thought it essential for teachers to expect students to be neat, on time, and polite, compared to 88 percent of the public. Only about a fifth agreed with the public that teachers should stress correct spelling, grammar, and punctuation. Only 37 percent thought it essential for teachers to learn how to maintain an orderly classroom.

Teacher educators also differ from employers and other professions on measuring standards or even employing them at all. Employers use standardized multiple-choice examinations for hiring. So do selective colleges and graduate and professional schools

---

12. Ann Bradley, "Survey Reveals Teens Yearn for High Standards," *Education Week* (February 12, 1997): 38–39, and J. Johnson and S. Farkas, *Getting By: What American Teenagers Really Think about Their Schools* (New York: Public Agenda, 1997).

13. Harris Interactive, *The MetLife Survey of the American Teacher 2001: Key Elements of Quality Schools* (New York, 2001).

14. S. Farkas and J. Johnson, *Different Drummers: How Teachers of Teachers View Public Education* (New York: Public Agenda, 1997).

for admission decisions. Such examinations are required for licensing in law, medicine, pharmacy, and other fields, because they are objective, efficient, and reliable. Yet 78 percent of teacher educators wanted less reliance on objective examinations.

Nearly two-thirds of teacher educators admitted that their programs often fail to prepare candidates for teaching in the real world, but only 4 percent reported that their programs typically dismiss students unsuitable for teaching. Thus, even starting with their undergraduate education, many prospective teachers are exposed to disparaging views of standards, incentives, and individual accomplishments.

As revealed by analysis of assigned readings in education courses, their preparation for teaching emphasizes:

- the notion that "authentic learning" only arises from "intrinsic motivation" in which student preferences rather than curriculum and course requirements dominate the choice of what and how to learn;

- an indifference or hostility to specifying objectives and measuring results;

- a view that children cannot learn until the "teachable moment" or until the "developmentally appropriate" time;

- a devaluing of knowledge (since "you can always look it up");

- an insistence that students should discover or "construct" their own understanding rather than being taught; and

- the idea that comprehension must be "socially constructed" in peer groups rather than taught or individually acquired.[15]

---

15. See J. E. Stone, "Developmentalism: An Obscure but Pervasive Restriction on Educational Improvement," *Education Policy Analysis Archives* 4, no. 8 (April 1996), http://epaa.asu.edu/epaa/v4n8.html. On student-centered learning, progressivism, and constructivism, see also Martin Kozloff, "Fad, Fraud, and Folly in Education," http://people.uncw.edu/kozloffm/fads.html and George K. Cunningham, "Education Schools: Helping or Hindering Potential Teachers," http://www.johnlocke.org/acro bat/pope_articles/cunninghameducationschools.pdf. For similar results from analyses of education course syllabi at elite schools of education, see David Steiner, "Skewed

These views may be characterized as "constructivism" rather than "instructivism." Instructivism implies that the teacher employs well-defined objectives, planned lessons, definite subject matter, explicit assessment of student progress, and, if necessary, re-teaching and additional practice until students master the objectives. Indeed, as documented in subsequent chapters, these views are corroborated by huge amounts of research on learning.

IMPRACTICAL EDUCATIONAL IDEAS

Instructivism descended from Aristotle, John Locke, Anglo-American pragmatic philosophy, and the findings of behavioral psychology. It is consistent with common sense and what most people think educators should do. The origins of constructivist views, on the other hand, may be traced to European Continental philosophy, including ideas that would seem absurd in modern empirical psychology. They include Plato's idea of "anamnesis," that the soul is immortal and repeatedly incarnated, implying that "all learning is but remembrance" requiring only maturation and possibly questions or reminders from teachers. Other odd views derived in the constructivist tradition are:

- Jean-Jacques Rousseau's notion of children born as "noble savages" only to be corrupted by adult society's influences;

- the Swiss child psychologist Piaget's view of developmental stages that proceed in a fixed sequence little influenced by teaching and practice;

- the followers of philosopher John Dewey who see schooling as social problem solving; and

---

Perspective" *Education Next* 5, no. 1 (Winter 2005), http://www.hoover.org/publications/ednext/3252116.html.

- British Marxists who think that the teaching of isolated knowledge and skills is bourgeoisie society's means of social class reproduction by denying the masses the big picture of social-class conflict.

Among highly influential contemporary descendents of the constructivist tradition is Alfie Kohn, who opposes education standards, homework, testing, and incentives. Another is Howard Gardner, who holds that various types of intelligence such as artistic, musical, and kinesthetic rather than direct teaching, practice, and incentives chiefly determine learning.[16] "Whole language" advocates dismiss the many studies that show that beginning readers greatly benefit from learning phonics (the sounding out of unfamiliar words from their letters). These language constructivists slight spelling, grammar, capitalization, and punctuation but emphasize student reactions and feelings about texts.[17]

Constructivists dismiss the practice of skills as "drill and kill." According to two eminent cognitive psychologists and a Nobel laureate in economics, however, the evidentiary basis of such constructivist theory consists largely of proponents who cite one another's values and opinions rather than rigorous evidence. But, as the psychologists write,

Nothing flies more in the face of the last 20 years of research than the assertion that practice is bad. All evidence, from the laboratory and from extensive case studies of professionals, indicates that real competence only comes with extensive practice. By denying the critical role of practice, one is denying children the very thing they need to achieve competence.[18]

16. See, for example, Alfie Kohn's *The Case Against Standardized Testing: Raising the Scores, Ruining the Schools* (New York: Heinemann, 2000) and Howard Gardner's *Intelligence Reframed: Multiple Intelligences for the 21st Century* (New York: Basic Books, 1999).

17. Louisa C. Moats, *Whole Language Lives On: The Illusion of "Balanced Reading" instruction* (Washington, DC: Thomas B. Fordham Foundation, 2000).

18. John R. Anderson, L. M. Reder, and Herbert A. Simon, "Radical Constructivism and Cognitive Psychology" in *Brookings Papers on Education Policy, 1998,* editor

Much current education theory is ill informed about scientific psychology, often drawing faddishly on "pop" psychology. It contradicts well-evidenced behavioral insights. As the subsequent chapters show, the facts support the value of instructivism, which calls on educators to have clear goals, plan effective activities to attain them, and measure student progress.

OVERVIEW

Drawing on psychological and economic research, the subsequent chapters describe how students learn and the best conditions for their learning. Chapter 2, "Causes of Learning," explains the evidence. Chapter 3, "Learning Principles," defines the alterable factors that psychologists have found consistently associated with high levels of learning—child-rearing practices, and the amount and quality of instruction, which are explained in subsequent chapters.

Chapter 4, "Families," is devoted to parents because they exert such a powerful influence on learning. In the first 18 years of life, children spend only about 8 percent of their time in school. Therefore, psychological conditions in the 92 percent of the time for which parents are chiefly responsible greatly influence what students learn.

Chapter 5, "Incentives," points out that K–12 educators often assume that students' motivation and self-esteem are principal determinants of how much students learn. The evidence, however, indicates that incentives such as encouragement and praise, high standards, and even money can exert powerful influences on what students learn. Though definitive efficacy evidence is unavailable, incentives also appear to influence teacher behavior. Bonuses can be used to recruit teachers into hard-to-staff fields such as mathematics and science and into schools that may be difficult to staff

Diane Ravitch (Washington, DC: Brookings Institution, 1998), 227–255 (quote from page 241).

such as those in high poverty areas. More generally, policy makers are beginning to use bonuses as incentives for teachers to induce greater student learning.

Chapter 6, "Teachers," summarizes the evidence on teacher credentials. Though most public school teachers are licensed and paid for education degrees and experience, these credentials have little or no effect on their students' learning. Their knowledge of subject matter appears more important.

Chapter 7, "Classroom Practices," explains teacher's classroom practices that make a difference. In addition to research on classrooms, findings on adult and technical education are also summarized because research in these fields has been rigorous and appears applicable to K–12 schooling. Because the findings were obtained from research on adults, moreover, the principles are applicable to educators themselves who seem needful of new learning, particularly teaching by means of new technologies, which are playing an increasingly larger role in schools.

Chapter 8, "School Policies," describes the psychological characteristics of safe, welcoming schools. Also described are the features that school principals and other leaders can incorporate into a school's organization, curriculum, and instruction to accelerate learning.

Chapter 9, "New Technologies," describes promising new technologies. Computers have already begun to change schools and are likely to continue at accelerating rates. It is possible even now to identify computer-based technologies that facilitate more effective learning than conventional methods and that allow students to learn equally well but more conveniently while saving school costs and students' time. Internet-based repositories and teaching programs can provide appropriate content and instruction. New social technologies enhance cooperation among educators, parents, and students.

Chapter 10, "Creative Destruction," ends the book with a look to the future. Effective instructional practices, school choice, and new "disruptive technologies" have separately produced better learning gains; they are the keys to improved learning. Used together they have the competitive potential to force large, bureaucratic, and repeatedly failing public schools to reform or close.

THESIS

The status quo, public school establishment has long proven its incapacity for improving achievement; substantial and rising expenditures have led nowhere. Psychology supports neither the beliefs nor the practices prevailing in public schools.

The most promising step is to foster new, competitive school organizations that efficiently integrate technologies that enhance one another and embody effective psychological principles of learning. In the United States, for example, 24 state-level virtual charter schools already incorporated computer and Internet technologies. The most compelling example, however, lies in Sweden which, beginning in 1993, has provided vouchers for all parents to choose public, parochial, and independent schools, an innovation that raised national achievement.

Though unexpected, Swedish for-profit schooling firms arose and thrived. For families with different educational preferences, they provided a diversity of choices. By setting examples of new technologies and market competition, they drove status quo schools to improve. The largest firm, called Knowledge Schools, quickly expanded, undoubtedly because its 30 campuses provide well-designed, new technologies that incorporate variations of the psychological principles explained in subsequent chapters. It allowed a level playing field of financial support. A few dozen such firms in the United States seem likely to do wonders to advance student achievement.

2

CAUSES OF LEARNING

Those who recommend substantial changes should be obliged to consider means and ends as well as causes and effects. Are the means ethical? Are the ends worthy, more valuable than other ends? When it strictly concerns their own affairs, adults in free societies should answer these philosophical questions for themselves and perhaps in consultation with those whose opinions they value. In the public sector, the questions may be answered by deliberation, voting, and by democratically governed institutions.

This book centers on an equally challenging question: Do the presumed means actually cause the ends in question, for this book, largely the attainment of achievement standards or academic learning? When there is little definitive evidence, however, other findings are cited. Psychologists, for example, cannot easily change child rearing, but they can study successful youngsters raised in adverse circumstances to discover behaviors of coaches, teachers, and other community members that may have helped them succeed despite their disadvantages.

Experiments

Experiments are sometimes called the "gold currency" in assessing causality. In K–12 education experiments, students are randomly assigned to one of several conditions or practices so that chance alone determines their group membership. At the end of the experiment, differences in outcomes are attributable to the condition or practice (in addition to presumably small chance differences between the groups).

Experiments in K–12 education are rare and, in this respect, education research is perhaps a century behind agriculture, the field in which experiments originated, which made astonishing increases in productivity. For the last quarter-century, large-scale, multi-site experiments increasingly provided solid evidence on the efficacy of new treatments in medicine. Since the 1950s, behavioral psychologists (those focused on observations and performance rather than feelings) conducted small-scale experiments in laboratories and classrooms.[1] With an annual budget of more than $600 million, the National Board for Educational Sciences is giving experiments high priority.

Experiments may be particularly valuable when they challenge strongly held professional views in medicine and other fields. High blood glucose levels, for example, are indicators of diabetes, and physicians have long assumed that lowering the levels to normal with medications or injected insulin would reduce heart attacks, amputations, and other outcomes. Three recent randomized experiments challenge that assumption and even suggest that reducing glucose from moderately high to strictly normal levels can actually be harmful.[2]

---

1. See Rena F. Subotnik and Herbert J. Walberg, editors, *The Scientific Basis of Educational Productivity* (Greenwich, CT: Information Age Publishers, 2006), sponsored by the American Psychological Association, for perspectives on experimental research.

2. Gary Taubes, "Paradoxical Effects of Tightly Controlled Blood Sugar," *Science*, 322, (October 2008): 365–367.

Experiments, of course, are not foolproof. By definition, students and educators in experiments are subject to contrived conditions, and experimental results may not be obtained in ordinary settings. Still, the results of experimental research are given special weight in this book, especially when they have been repeated and field-tested in a wide variety of settings.

Generally, the next best basis of causal evidence is quasi-experiments or statistically controlled studies in which students who have been conventionally or naturally assigned to conditions or practices are compared with respect to their learning outcomes, and statistical methods are employed in an effort to remove any pre-existing differences among the groups.

Quasi-experiments are much easier to conduct than experiments because they are less disruptive of schools and other organizations. They do not require, as experiments do, special random assignment of students. They do require, however, the often-questionable but possibly testable assumption that pre-existing and concurrent differences among the groups and their conditions are insignificant.

In such non-experimental, statistically controlled studies, it is especially important to take into consideration any pre-existing differences in achievement among students and to measure the learning gains or progress made during the course of the study. Fortunately, hundreds of such studies were carried out in the last five decades and are available for synthesis. They form the largest basis of evidence in the subsequent chapters. A single study such as those featured in the press may prove little, but a few dozen studies conducted in many sites and circumstances, most of which come to the same conclusion, should be taken very seriously.

Less formal, observational research can sometimes serve as a basis of evidence, especially when immediate and substantial effects can be observed. The Wright brothers, for example, did not contrast experimental planes with control planes. Rather they tinkered with the shape of the wings in efforts to determine what would yield the greatest lift.

Similarly, behavioral psychologists use incentives, rewards, or what they call "reinforcement" to produce desired changes in behavior. Small-scale studies of a single person, for example, contrast the amount of desired behavior observed in reinforced conditions compared to base rates over a number of periods. Large-scale studies may also show strong reinforcement effects. In a study described in a subsequent chapter, for example, the number of inner-city Dallas high school students passing Advanced Placement courses increased by a factor of roughly ten when they and their teachers were each paid $100 for each Advanced Placement, college-level examination passed.

Research Synthesis

None of the research methods described above are fail-safe; all are subject to causal uncertainties. To arrive at recommendations for education policies and practices, this book synthesizes the conclusions in the corpus of largely psychological evidence brought together in two ways. The first is to statistically analyze the results of many studies of the same practice (a method called "meta-analysis"). If, for example, 85 percent of the studies of an educational practice show a positive effect, it may be concluded that the practice generally works and can be recommended. Going a step further, such syntheses yield an overall quantitative result called an "effect size," and practices that yield the greatest effects can be recommended over others. Of course, other criteria such as practicality and costs must be weighed.[3]

---

3. In contrast to the social sciences, medicine and psychology more often make use of meta-analysis since many independent studies of a single practice are available for summary. It is possible to calculate separately the effects of more and less rigorous studies, of variations and degrees of treatments, and human subjects such as males

A second method for synthesizing research is to review reports by specialized experts who have invested decades of their time into mastering special fields of education such as tutoring and computer-based instruction. Such experts are generally familiar not only with these methods of research, but with the special problems and proposed solutions in their fields. Experts, of course, are fallible even when they agree. Drawing blood to restore the balance of body humors, for example, was once standard medical practice and may have killed George Washington.

Atypical Outliers

Child rearing is obviously an important cause of learning but one in which it is extremely difficult to carry out rigorous long-term research. Families understandably want to preserve their privacy, and research interveners cannot easily change child-rearing preferences and habits. In view of these and other difficulties, studies of atypical cases contrasting success and failure can be suggestive if not definitive in identifying the conditions of childhood success despite adverse circumstances.

A good example is the investigation of "resilient" or "hardy" children who grow up successfully under adverse conditions. For example, a classic and influential study traced Hawaiian children born in 1955. A high-risk sample was selected for the presence of multiple risk factors during the first two years of the child's life that predict child, adolescent, and adult failures. The early risk factors included prenatal stress, poverty, family discord, and inadequate parental education.

About a third of the high-risk group was designated resilient

---

and females. Strong effects are often found to be "robust," that is, they work well across various kinds of studies, but this tendency should be investigated rather than assumed.

because, when older, they were more responsible, mature, and more socially integrated than their less resilient at-risk peers. Continuing assessments showed they had good relations with their caregivers and more attention and less separation from them, better physical health, and exposure to fewer life stressors. Perhaps the most significant finding was that such resilient children had a long-term, close relation with a caring, responsible adult other than a parent such as an aunt, uncle, teacher, or coach.[4]

Other resilience studies[5] have been made of children of mentally ill parents and teenage mothers, those in economic hardship, institutions, or foster care, and severely maltreated and chronically ill. The characteristics of such children that predict resilience are effective parenting; sustained child connections with competent adults other than parents; the child's appeal to people, particularly adults who can constructively guide them; intellectual skills; areas of accomplishment valued by themselves and others; hopefulness; religious faith and affiliation; socioeconomic advantages; effective community agencies; and kind fortune.

Adults who guide such resilient children tend to make them feel worthwhile and valued; exhibit competence for emulation; provide guidance and constructive feedback; support the undertaking of appropriate new challenges; function as door-opening advocates; and provide competence- and confidence-building experiences. Of course, resilient children may have only one or a few of these advantages. Unfortunately, schools have little control of these aspects of children's character and lives, or of adults in the community who can exercise such practices. Extremely resilient children are rare by definition as are the adults who help them through voluntary, continuing, and patient acts, which may be difficult to repeat widely.

---

4. Emmy E. Werner and R. S. Smith, *Overcoming the Odds: High Risk Children from Birth to Adulthood* (Ithaca, NY: Cornell University Press, 1992).

5. Ann S. Masten, "Resilience in Individual Development: Successful Adaptation Despite Risk and Adversity" in *Educational Resilience in the Inner City America*, M. C. Wang and E. W. Gordon, editors (Hillsdale, NJ: Lawrence Erlbaum, 1994).

Even more difficult would be enacting such behaviors in public schools that are increasingly large, departmentalized, and impersonal and that in large cities often serve mobile children in poverty who frequently lack the personal traits and advantages associated with resilience. Perhaps the biggest challenge for researchers is the possibility of reverse causality. Resilient children may have cheerful personalities, good looks, persevering engagement, and other winning characteristics that elicit encouraging, supportive, long-term behavior from adults. In which direction does causality flow?

Like atypical children, atypical schools may also yield information that provides suggestive evidence. As mentioned in subsequent chapters, examples include studies of schools with high concentrations of children in poverty who achieve well. It is reasonable to ask what practices set such schools apart from high-poverty failing schools. If this evidence is corroborated by other research, practical implications may be drawn to be evaluated in practice.

Much of life follows such scientifically questionable conclusions. Many findings in psychology and the social sciences remain uncertain and controversial; these fields cannot serve as definitive and comprehensive guides to life. Not knowing what is best, it often seems promising to follow successful examples. The underlying causes are often unscientifically grounded, but they may be practical when accompanied by skepticism, when they are analogous with better-evidenced conclusions from related circumstances, and when the results are continuously evaluated.

3

PRINCIPLES OF LEARNING

Following Aristotle, learning may be considered the development of associations, mainly of ideas but also behaviors and feelings. Learning implies the acquisition and association of ideas from the environment and their recall into conscious memory. Creativity (including problem solving) is the trial-and-error search for novel and useful solutions through combinations of stored ideas and external stimuli.

The amount and rate of learning varies among students, as precocity illustrates at one extreme. As Sternberg and Davidson conclude, "Precocious children form connections at a much more rapid rate than do ordinary children, and exceptional adults have formed exceptionally large numbers of variegated stimulus-response connections."[1]

Children and adults require time for the acquisition and association of elements, but well-organized environments can accelerate learning far beyond conventional bounds. Ericksson, Chase, and Faloon,[2] for example, showed that an undergraduate of average

---

1. Robert J. Sternberg and Janet E. Davidson, "Cognitive Development in Gifted and Talented" in *The Gifted and Talented*, F. D. Horowitz and M. O'Brien, editors (Washington, DC: American Psychological Association, 1985), 44.
2. K. Anders Ericsson, William G. Chase, and S. Faloon, "Acquisition of a Memory Skill," *Science* 208, no. 11 (1980): 81–82.

intelligence, given 230 hours (about six 40-hour weeks) of special instruction and practice, raised his memory for numbers from 7 to 79 digits—larger than stage performers with astonishing memories for numbers and 9 times larger than that taken by psychologists as indicative of superior quantitative intelligence. An avid runner, the student associated number strings with running times.

This experiment with a single subject illustrates the potential of intensive, directed instruction in a highly specialized skill. Like other learning, of course, such extraordinary acquisition may not carry over to other knowledge and skills (what psychologists call transfer). So, such a memory feat could not be expected to have helped the runner with weight lifting or calculus.

Usually, the difference between beginners and experts is the amount of time they have spent in engaged practice, particularly "chunking," or grouping elements they have learned into easily, confidently, and quickly processed clusters or "chunks." A chess master sees a few major chunks or patterns of chess pieces on a board where a novice sees a dozen individual pieces related in a huge number of ways. Because of speedy processing of chunked information, the master can beat a dozen good players played simultaneously.

Based on such insight, the polymath psychologist and economics Nobel Laureate Herbert Simon condensed large amounts of psychological research into an elegant, practical formulation that explains many findings about learning, expertise, and discovery. He estimates that expert mastery of a field requires 50,000 specialized chunks, the number of words in a college-educated reader's recognition vocabulary. The highest mastery may require a million chunks, representing concentrated study for a decade of 70-hour weeks, even for the most talented individual. There are occasional exceptions, like Bobby Fisher and Mozart, who managed to attain the highest mastery in chess and music composition in seven to nine years.[3]

---

3. Herbert A. Simon, *Sciences of the Artificial* (Cambridge: MIT Press, 1981).

As Simon explains, chunking and the association of internal and external elements underlie thought processes from childhood learning to the highest accomplishments. Experts have paid the price of their time, concentration, and other forgone opportunities. The other limiting factor, according to Simon, is the number of items of information, perhaps 2 to 7, that can be held in conscious memory long enough to associate or transfer to long-term memory, which may take 5 to 10 seconds. The more expert people become in chess, science, and other fields, the more information they keep in permanent memory and, even more critically, the more efficiently they relate new to old information.

Information in the mind of an expert, moreover, is more thoroughly indexed and therefore more easily and quickly accessed by conscious short-term memory. Within the index, information elements are elaborately linked together so that information can be recalled through various associations even when parts of the index are forgotten. Whether consciously or not, experts elaborately index learned material and make it rapidly accessible by means-ends or trial-and-error searches. Such indexing serves the expert even in advanced problem solving, when nearly forgotten information must be retrieved.

Anders Ericsson summarized psychological research on top performance in the arts, billiards, chess, golf, musical composition and performance, telegraphy, typing, science, sports, and surgery.[4] Aside from long hours of practice, the top performers continually stretched themselves, usually for at least a decade, giving their full concentration to correcting their weaknesses and continually integrating new knowledge and skills into their repertoires. Not satisfied with mere excellence, they kept breaking new barriers. For this reason, to become a merely excellent performer in modern times

---

4. K. Anders Ericsson, "The Influence of Experience and Deliberate Practice on the Development of Superior Expert Performance," in *Cambridge Handbook of Expertise and Expert Performance*, K. Anders Ericsson, Neil Charness, Robert R. Hoffman, Paul J. Feltovich, editors, (Cambridge, U.K.: Cambridge University Press, 2006).

requires performance levels considered unattainable a decade or two ago.

A Model of Learning

Figure 1 is an abstraction of learning processes. Information from the teacher, other means of instruction, or uncontrived experience may gain attention. Previously learned or recorded information may also arise. The elements of information may be combined to answer a question or solve a problem.

Recycling in these ways works well, particularly if repeated many times. It can lead to "automaticity" so that the learner no longer needs to reconstruct knowledge acquired earlier. Historically interpreted as a mark of genius, "keeping at it" promotes such efficiency. One of Lord Chesterfield's letters to his son advised,

FIGURE 1
A Simplified Model of Learning

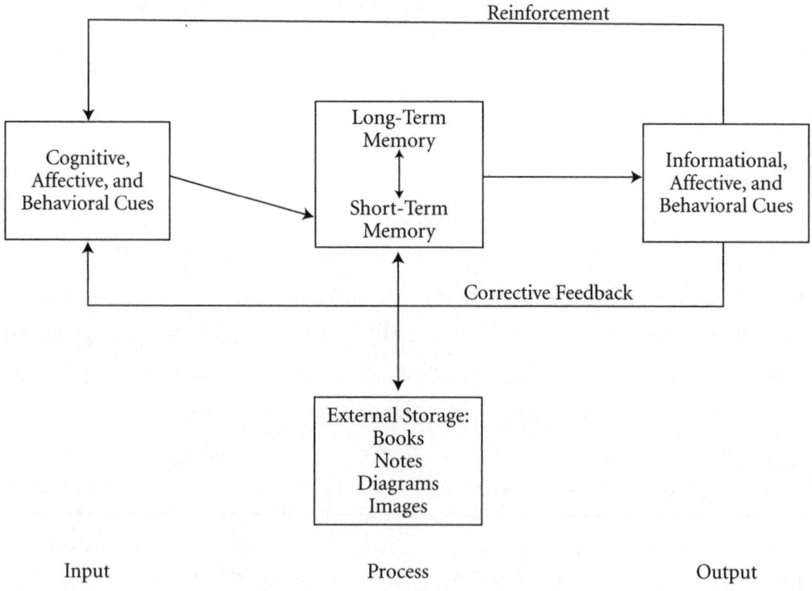

> Steady and undissipated attention to one object, is a sure mark
> of a superior genius; as hurry, bustle, and agitation, are the
> never failing symptoms of a weak and frivolous mind.[5]

On learning and discovery, William James similarly wrote,

> The sustained attention of the genius, sticking to his subject
> for hours together, is for the most part of the passive sort. The
> minds of geniuses are full of copious and original associations.
> The subject of thought, once started, develops all sorts of fasci-
> nating consequences. The attention is led along one of these to
> another in the most interesting manner, and the attention
> never once tends to stray away.[6]

So much for the claims about "multitasking."

Distractions, moreover, such as misbehaving classmates in
school and the common buzz or clamor of television and other
disturbances in the home, can result in inefficient recycling. Isolat-
ing study carrels in universities and in Japanese homes are classic
solutions. Computer-assisted instruction may reduce distractions
by monitors that fill much of the field of vision and headphones
that diminish stray noise (though unrestricted Internet surfing may
be more distracting).

As exemplified in learning a first or additional language,
appropriate repetition and re-teaching of the material to be learned
is crucial. Common words such as "I," "you," "is," and "are" are
usually learned most rapidly and securely not only because they
are short but because they are so often repeated in speaking. In
classrooms, drilling learners on indispensable knowledge and skills

---

5. Philip Dormer Stanhope, Earl of Chesterfield, *Letters to His Son: On the Fine
Art of Becoming a Man of the World and a Gentleman*, (Oliver H. G. Leigh, editor),
(Washington, D.C.: M. W. Dunne, 1901), Letter IX, London, April 14, O.S. 1747, page
15, online at: http://books.google.com/books?id = 1rHhELIw4usC&printsec = front
cover&dq = earl + of + chesterfield%27s + letters&source = gbs_similarbooks_r&cad = 2#
v = onepage&q = &f = false

6. William James, *Talks to Teachers*, (New York: Henry Holt, 1899), http://www.des
.emory.edu/mfp/tt11.html.

until they reach confident mastery promotes their efficiency in more advanced learning. In some cases, quick "automaticity" is critical; learners who must think about the difference between the letters "b" and "d" are unlikely to readily comprehend prose.

Reinforcement and Correctives

Time investments alone are unlikely to suffice. As Figure 1 indicates, reinforcement and correctives make practice efficient because they provide knowledge of results. For correct or appropriate responses, reinforcement or effective application of appropriate incentives can encourage learners in the short or long term. Some may benefit from praise or simply seeing that their teacher is pleased with what they have done; others may find it reinforcing merely to know they have made a step toward their long-term goal of becoming a doctor.

Reinforcement and correctives work best if they are quickly furnished as in the case of homework and tests that are promptly graded or marked, and returned. To increase cycling speed much faster, students may be taught to evaluate the quality of their own responses.

As illustrated on the left of Figure 1, instructional cues may be equally critical. One key to their success is their appropriateness for individual learners. A common dilemma of teaching a whole class at a time is that some students already know the material over which others have insufficient knowledge to master. New computer technologies help solve this problem by continuously assessing what individuals know and need to know. Well-developed systems provide immediate, high-quality instructional reinforcement and corrective cues. They hold the promise of much more efficient learning.

Another kind of appropriateness is meaningful content. It may be extremely difficult, for example, to learn some things without the prerequisite meaning imparted by prior knowledge. For more than a century, psychologists showed that nonsense syllables such as "vaqtz" and sentences composed of them that lack meaning are much more difficult to learn than those expressed in meaningful terms. Similarly, it may be vastly difficult to learn multiplication before addition, or the causes of the Civil War without some understanding of prior American history. Since new learning depends on prior knowledge and skills, the appropriate choice, organization, and sequence of curriculum content can help make teaching and learning efficient.

Some aspects of content such as sequences of seemingly arbitrary names are not meaningful. Memory aids, however, that "chunk" such arbitrary material can speed learning. The sentence, for example, "Mary's Violet Eyes Make John Sit Up Nights Proposing" helps students remember the order of the planets, Mercury, Venus, Earth, Mars, and so on. Medical students make use of similar aids in mastering the vast amount of material they must learn to become a doctor, one of the most demanding of all occupations.

The appropriate and extensive recycling of the elements in Figure 1 can, over time, generate astonishing results. One extremely difficult task is learning to speak a new language fluently, a feat that few accomplish in adult life. Yet, children the world over attain first-language fluency with apparent ease. Few adults past college age willingly subject themselves to the time, effort, and correctives required. Even after much contrived study, most adults are hard-pressed to achieve a child's level of fluency.

Adults do not lack intelligence but engagement in the new language that children are afforded in much of their day. Contrived or not, immersive and enduring language and other environments strongly shape accomplishments; societies and individuals, moreover, can choose or determine their environments.

Language learning also illustrates the power of recycling compared not only to age but even intelligence. From its inception, intelligence measurement centered on vocabulary and other closely related first-language skills. For this reason, on a Swahili or Urdu intelligence test, most American youngsters and adults would score at the level of an infant.

Children and adult newcomers to challenging fields may feel daunted by the sustained engagement required for mastery. Fortunately, competence in most subjects and fields only requires a fraction of the expert's effort. An hour or two a day may permit average American school children, who currently dedicate four to five hours a day to television viewing, to achieve reasonable competence in fields such as chess, sports, second languages, and playing musical instruments. More hours a day can lead to impressive results as exemplified by American children who spend a year in a family and community where English is rarely spoken and, as a consequence, become fluent in a second language.

These principles of learning have been established in psychological laboratories, and they have been increasingly corroborated in K–12 classroom research. They are appealing for two reasons: They causally affect learning, and parents, educators, and policy makers may alter them to advance achievement. One factor, however, has been given too much emphasis—ability, which is discussed briefly in the next section.

ABILITY

In a monograph, "The Economics and Psychology of Personality Traits," a team of economists and psychologists[7] collected the results of many studies of the relations of psychological traits and a

---

7. Lex Borghans, Angela Lee Duckworth, James J. Heckman, and Bas ter Weel, "The Economics and Psychology of Personality Traits" (Cambridge, MA: National Bureau of Economic Research, February 2008) Working Paper 13810. The two next most predictive traits are conscientiousness, which predicted only 4 percent of the variation in grades, and openness to experience, which accounted for 1 percent of the variation in years of education. As the authors point out, personality traits often lack stability and are often unreliably measured.

variety of outcomes. Childhood intelligence was the best predictor of educational outcomes, but it predicted only 20 percent of the variation in college grades and 30 percent of the variation in years of education. These figures indicate that intelligence weakly predicts these outcomes, and that less intelligent students can exceed those with higher intelligence. Other factors such as the families, incentives, and the quality and amount of learning time are not only more powerful but also more readily alterable.

Another problem with intelligence is that psychologists do not agree on what it is or how to measure it. One view, for example, is that a "g-factor," sometimes thought to be the speed of mental processing, underlies all other mental abilities, but other views maintain there are many, up to several hundred, intelligence factors.[8] Psychologists and others, moreover, have engaged in a long, voluminous, and unconstructive controversy over the relative weights of heredity and environment, but, in any case, most agree that intelligence cannot be readily altered.

For these reasons, ability has little priority in this book. One psychometric measure—prior level of achievement in subject matter—is given a section of a chapter for an important reason. Instruction should be suited to the student's knowledge and skills.

---

8. For a discussion of various views, see David G. Geary, *The Origin of Mind: Evolution of Brain Cognition and General Intelligence* (Washington, DC: American Psychological Association, 2005) and John B. Carroll, *Human Cognitive Abilities* (New York: Cambridge University Press, 1993).

4

Families

I n his 1948 Harvard lectures *Social Class Influences on Learning*,[1] Allison Davis described the link between family circumstances and school learning. The largest study of kindergarteners ever made[2] confirmed this link. The study showed that children's reading and mathematics examination scores varied greatly and that the lower their socioeconomic status, the poorer their scores even before they started first grade. These differences persist and, paraphrasing the poet Gerard Manley Hopkins, it can be said the child is the parent of the adult.

Though not causally definitive, the largest national student survey ever carried out brought public and legislative attention to family influences. Commissioned by the U.S. Congress, James S. Coleman and his colleagues conducted the survey, "Equality of Educational Opportunity." They questioned 645,000 students to investigate possible gaps in school opportunity and achievement. The report concluded,

---

1. Allison Davis, *Social-Class Influences on Learning.* (Cambridge, MA: Harvard University Press, 1948).

2. Valerie E. Lee and David Burkam, *Inequality at the Starting Gate* (Washington, DC: Economic Policy Institute, 2002).

One implication stands out above all: That schools bring little influence to bear on a child's achievement that is independent of his [sic, or her] background and general social context; and that this very lack of independent effect means that the inequalities imposed on children by their home, neighborhood, and peer environment are carried along to become inequalities with which they confront in adult life at the end of school.[3]

Nearly a quarter-century later, Coleman reflected: "The analysis showed what had already been well known: the powerful relation of the child's own family characteristics to his (or her) achievement, a relation stronger than any school factors."[4]

Coleman's conclusions have held up well and have been explained by the parents' behaviors that affect their children. In 2001, for example, Caroline Hoxby reported that 94 percent of the variance of children's mathematics achievement scores is explained by such family variables as parents' education, their attendance at school events, course planning with their children, knowing graduation requirements, taking family museum visits, and having more than 50 books in the home. (Hoxby's 94 percent figure is not far from the 92 percent of time children spend outside school in the first 18 years of life by my calculations.) Hoxby estimated that neighborhood characteristics such as mean household income explained 4 percent of the variance in achievement, leaving only 3 percent explained by such school characteristics as per-student spending, class sizes, and teacher salaries.[5]

A caveat: Policy makers and educators ought not to toss up their hands in view of these findings. Parental behavior can be altered.

3. James S. Coleman, Ernest Q. Campbell, C. J. Hobson, James McPartland, Alexander M. Mood, Frederick D. Weinfeld, and Robert L. York, *Equality of Educational Opportunity* (Washington, DC: U.S. Office of Education, 1966), 325.

4. James S. Coleman, *Equality and Achievement in Education* (Boulder, CO: Westview Press, 1990).

5. Caroline M. Hoxby, "If Families Matter Most, Where do Schools Come In?" in *A Primer on America's Schools,* Terry M. Moe, editor (Stanford, CA: Hoover Institution Press, 2001), 89–126. Because of rounding, the figures total 101 percent.

Some jurisdictions are considering not only parent education programs but parent pay for changed behavior and increased achievement. During the course of a year, moreover, an excellent teacher can increase learning so substantially that it can positively affect learning over several subsequent years. Over the dozen years of a students' elementary and secondary schooling, superior teaching by itself might remove the usual demographic achievement gaps. Even so, the deleterious effects of family poverty must be acknowledged.

POVERTY EFFECTS

Helping children in poverty or of lower socioeconomic status learn continues to be a major concern. Socioeconomic status is usually indicated by parent income, education, and occupation. Parent behavior, however, is generally much greater in its effect on achievement than socioeconomic status. Parental behavior, moreover, can change, whereas demographic factors such as income are usually more stable. Though this chapter discusses demography further, it concentrates more on programs that constructively modify the parent behaviors that affect children's learning.

Psychologists have rigorously studied the family factors related to school failure in poor families, 20 of which are shown in Table 1. Some factors occur before birth and are manifested in low birth weight. Others begin at birth and continue to influence the child during the school years, affecting the child's ability to cope with stress and delay gratification.

One big difference between parents of different levels of socioeconomic status (SES) in preparing children for school showed up in preschoolers' recorded playtime conversations. Children from 12 to 14 months of age showed insignificant vocabulary differences, but by age 3, welfare children had vocabularies of roughly 500 words, middle/lower SES children about 700, and higher SES children 1,100 words, more than double the vocabulary of welfare children.

These vocabulary differences were strongly connected to

TABLE 1
Poverty-Related Factors That Impede Achievement

A. **Prenatal and perinatal factors**
   1. Stress and disease
   2. Premature birth
   3. Low birth weight

B. **Family status**
   4. Adolescent parenthood
   5. Single parenthood

C. **Divorce and frequent parental consequences**
   6. Depression
   7. Anxiety
   8. Irritability
   9. Decreased income
   10. Lowered self-esteem

D. **Frequent moving**
   11. Residence
   12. Schools

E. **Child rearing**
   13. Fewer verbal interchanges between parents and children
   14. Less exposure to stimulating vocabulary
   15. Punitive practices
   16. Less praise and affection
   17. Provision of poor problem-solving strategies

F. **Resulting child problems:**
   18. Inability to cope with stress and frustration
   19. Incapacity to postpone gratification
   20. Poor readiness for reading

parent behaviors in the home. Higher SES parents talked more often with their children and spoke about 2,000 words per hour. Welfare parents spoke only about 500 words per hour to their children. By age 4, a child in a professional family would have heard an estimated 45 million words, compared to the 26 million of a working-class child, and 13 million of a welfare child.

In addition, higher SES parents used a wider variety of words, more complicated sentences, more verb tenses, and more sentence types. They gave their children more positive feedback and interacted with them more during each hour they were together. In fact, the higher SES parents gave their children encouraging feedback an estimated 750,000 times by age 4, a total of 6 times more often than welfare parents. Welfare parents gave 2.2 times more negative, discouraging feedback than affluent parents. Parenting behaviors such as these predicted about 60 percent of the vocabulary sizes of three-year-olds.[6]

Other studies[7] show that middle-class parents tend to expect their children to achieve more and often help them do it. Lower SES mothers, on the other hand, tend to do tasks for their children rather than teaching them how to do them for themselves, thus neglecting development of their problem-solving skills. They less often expect their children to do well and view schools as inaccessible places where they have little control, which does little to aid their children's school performance. In addition, home observations show lower SES homes lack parental involvement, play materials, discipline, and an organized environment, all linked to higher reading achievement.

PRESCHOOL PROGRAMS

This chapter on families discusses preschool programs because the child's experiences before school have been and are often still considered the responsibility of families rather than schools. Even so, it should be acknowledged that families have changed in recent decades. The percentages of teen, unwed, and working mothers rose, and federal and state government programs played a larger role in young child rearing and preparation for schooling.

To be better prepared for kindergarten and first grade, lower SES children need better academic preparation, but do preschool programs improve their prospects? An analysis of 48 published articles examining the effects of early childhood interventions suggests slight positive effects overall.[8] Nonrandomized studies indicated

---

6. Betty Hart and Todd R. Risley, *Meaningful Differences In The Everyday Experience Of Young American Children* (Baltimore: Paul H. Brooks, 1995).

7. Allen Wigfield and Steven R. Asher, "Social And Motivational Influences On Reading" in *Handbook of Reading Research* 1, P. David Pearson, Rebeccah Barr, Michael Kamil, and Peter L. Mosenthal, editors (New York: Longman, 1984), 423–452.

8. Marian J. Bakermans-Kranenburg, Marinus H van Ijzendoorn, and Robert H. Bradley, "Those Who Have, Receive: The Matthew Effect in Early Childhood Intervention in the Home Environment," *Review of Educational Research* no. 1, 75, (2005): 1–26.

highly inflated effect sizes, with an average of 0.58, which is spectac-
ularly misleading since randomized experiments show a tiny effect
of 0.13, illustrating the tendency for rigorous field studies of social
programs to show smaller, often null effects. Preschools may simply
attract more competent and caring parents but bring little value to
them since their children may do well without preschool.

Even randomized studies may be causally misleading because
higher SES parents may more often keep their children in programs
rather than removing them. Confirming the Matthew effect (Figure
2), the programs may increase the advantages of already advantaged
children, leading to greater rather than smaller gaps and defeating
the egalitarian claims of preschool advocates.

Preschool program sessions, however, are often short and the
programs often continue for only a limited time, which may limit
their effects. Also, program characteristics such as a remote location
or insufficient publicity about availability may be such that lower
SES parents are less able to enroll their children.

The largest early childhood program is Head Start. President
Lyndon Johnson led the initiation of the program begun in 1965 to
help poverty-stricken children from birth till age five, and today,
900,000 children and their families participate each year. Head Start
supplies a wide range of services, including parent training and
vision, dental, nutritional, and health services.

A 1985 synthesis of roughly 300 weak Head Start studies
showed the apparent children's gains made in Head Start vanished
after only two or three years. Students did better on achievement
tests at the end of the program compared to control groups, but
soon the difference became trifling.[9] More recent studies have been
slightly more positive.[10]

---

9. Karl R. White, "Efficacy of Early Intervention," *Journal of Special Education* 19
(1985): 401–416.

10. Janet Currie, "Early Childhood Programs." *Journal of Economic Perspectives* 15
(2001): 213–238 and Lynn A. Karoly and Peter W. Greenwood, *Investing in our Children: What We Know and Don't Know about the Costs and Benefits of Early Childhood
Interventions* (Santa Monica, CA: RAND Corporation, 1998).

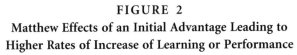

FIGURE 2
Matthew Effects of an Initial Advantage Leading to
Higher Rates of Increase of Learning or Performance

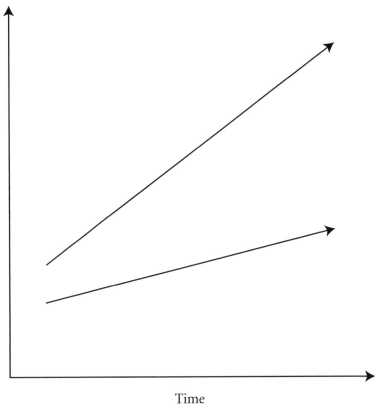

Time

The research firm Mathematica, for example, conducted a rigorous, large-scale, random assignment evaluation of a particular
Head Start program intended to improve children's health and
development as well as strengthen family and community partner-
ships and provide services to low-income families with pregnant
women, infants, and toddlers.[11] They found small but positive

_____

11. Mathematica Policy Research, Inc., *Early Head Start: Making a Difference in the
Lives of Infants and Toddlers and Their Families: The Impacts of Early Head Start.*
(Princeton, NJ, 2002).

impacts on parents and children through age three. The 17 program instances investigated included 3,001 families and showed small effect sizes in the .10 to .20 range. While these may be steps in the right direction, they are tiny and, if they are like other early childhood effects, may fade in a year or two.

An Academically Focused Program

A landmark investigation of the Chicago Child-Parent Centers (CPC), the only long-term study of an academically focused school-related program, showed noteworthy long-term impact and cost-effectiveness.[12] Starting with students at age three, the CPC provided teacher-directed, whole-class instruction and small-group activities focusing on language and pre-mathematical skills. The program provided parent resource rooms in each center to encourage parental participation and to change behavior at home.

Funded by the National Institutes of Health, the long-term study compared the 989 participating children to matched control group children and showed higher cognitive skills in kindergarten. Continuing later grades, the participants sustained higher achievement, and had significantly lower rates of special-education placement and grade retention than the control group, a 29 percent higher rate of school completion, and a 33 percent lower rate of juvenile arrest. At a per-child program cost of $6,730 for 18 months of part-day services, the estimated benefits per child through age 21 were $47,759 in improved economic well-being and reduced

---

12. Arthur J. Reynolds, *Success in Early Intervention: The Chicago Child-Parent Centers* (Lincoln, NE: University of Nebraska Press, 2000), and Arthur J. Reynolds and Judy A. Temple, "Long-term Effects of an Early Childhood Intervention on Educational Achievement and Juvenile Arrest: A 15 Year Follow-up of Low-income Children in Public Schools." *Journal of the American Medical Association* 285 (2001): 2339–2346; Arthur J. Reynolds and Judy A. Temple, "Cost-Effective Early Childhood Development Programs from Preschool to Third Grade," *Annual Review of Clinical Psychology* (March 2008): 79–91.

expenses for remediation. Few education studies have followed children as long or calculated the program costs and benefits.

What made this particular program so successful? The CPC program engaged parents in academically motivating home activities to teach their children numbers, letters, and colors. The program directly taught language skills aligned with the kindergarten curriculum of neighborhood schools in contrast to other early childhood programs that stress "developmental appropriateness," play, and self-esteem. Probably because most programs are unlike the CPC's, a review of early childhood program evaluations showed that roughly half had no impact on achievement.[13]

Benefits in Relation to Costs

The evaluation of the Child-Parent Centers program is further distinguished by its long-term study into adulthood and the measurement of monetary benefits in relation to costs. In 2008, the sample averaged 28 years of age, and it was estimated that each dollar invested in the preschool program appeared to save society $10 in the costs of special education, medical care, incarceration, and unemployment through early adulthood.

As indicated below, other preschool programs on average saved about $6 per invested dollar and were clearly superior to other investments in young children such as teacher and parent training, small classes in the early grades, intensive reading, tutoring, and full-day kindergarten.

As pointed out previously, however, the evaluations on which these estimates are based are subject to sizable uncertainties. Almost none of the evaluations were randomized experiments, and their apparent effects may have been caused by factors other than the

---

13. Lynn A. Karoly and Peter W. Greenwood, *Investing in our Children: What We Know and Don't Know about the Costs and Benefits of Early Childhood Interventions* (Santa Monica, CA: RAND Corporation, 1998).

TABLE 2
Program Effects

Childhood Program	Benefit/Cost Ratio
Preschool	6.02
"Women, Infants, and Children," a nutrition program for children up to five years old	3.14
"Skills, Opportunities, and Recognition," teacher and parent training to reduce delinquency and drug use in grades 1 through 6	3.07
Small classes in early grades	2.47
"Reading Recovery," an expensive tutoring program for children falling behind in reading	0.30
Full-day kindergarten	0.00

program. The programs, for example, may have simply attracted and retained families whose children would have done as well without the programs. Though quantitatively sophisticated, moreover, cost estimates of long-term effects depend on initial assumptions, which are usually questionable. Can analysts agree, for example, on society's or an individual's full cost of unemployment or a year in prison?

A Challenge to Radical Environmentalism

In *The Nurture Assumption*[14] and other writings, psychologist Judith Rich Harris concluded controversially that parent influences on their children are transmitted mainly through the genes rather than child-rearing practices. Her evidenced-based skepticism was met by members of the "therapeutic community" of psychologists, social

---

14. Judith Rich Harris, *The Nurture Assumption* (New York: The Free Press, 1998).

workers, and educators with allegations of social Darwinism, political incorrectness, and penury. Harris, however, answered her critics, persisted in accumulating evidence, and eventually won prizes
from distinguished groups including the largest scientific and professional group of psychologists in the world, the American Psychological Association.

Given all the evidence including that of Harris, it can be provi-
sionally concluded that preschool effects on achievement lasting
more than two years are plausible but unproven. While most preschool programs may have slight and temporary impact on learning, a few programs might be effective. Given the uncertainties, the
decisions about their use are best left to parents.

Governments and foundations, moreover, are unwise in
spending taxpayers' and donors' money on preschools without
incorporating evaluations of their possible efficacy. Researchers,
moreover, ought to seek to find the features of programs that do
work, which would require difficult, long-term, randomized multi-
site studies.

Parent Influences During the School Years

Home Environments

In Southern Ontario, Kevin Marjoribanks first showed that considerable variance in verbal ability can be accounted for by psychological assessments of the family environment. From home interviews
with parents in 1972, he rated the degree to which families encouraged achievement, activeness, intellectuality, and independence. A
composite of the ratings was substantially correlated (about .60)
with verbal ability tests.[15]

---

15. Kevin Marjoribanks, "Ethnic and Environmental Influences on Mental Abilities," *American Journal of Sociology* 78 (1972): 323–337.

A search of educational, psychological, and sociological literature turned up another 18 similar parent-interview studies of the association between home-environment measures and learning in samples totaling about 5,000 students in eight countries.[16] Correlations of intelligence, motivation, and achievement with indexes of parental stimulation of the student in the home are moderate. (Specifically, the medians of 92 simple and 62 multiple correlations of home environment and learning were respectively 0.37 and 0.44.)

These learning correlations are considerably higher than those involving SES (which average only 0.25).[17] Still, they are all correlational. As discussed in the introductory chapter, bright children might stimulate their parents to provide them with an academically stimulating home life. Nature as well as nurture may be another underlying cause of the correlations.

Behavioral Interventions in Homes

Roland Barth, on the other hand, uncovered 24 randomized in-home behavioral studies of short-term reinforcement of academic motivation and behavior—some including delinquents and children with home and school misbehavior problems such as inattentiveness and disruptiveness. The studies in the Barth review are rigorously experimental in the Skinnerian tradition. Start-up periods of daily or weekly teacher notes or checklists on classroom behavior and no reinforcement are followed by a period of home-administered consumables such as ice cream as well as earned privileges, and verbal praise geared to classroom performance. Reinforcement is phased in and out; behavior responds accordingly, and is therefore said to be under experimental control.[18]

---

16. Barbara K. Iverson and Herbert J. Walberg, "Home Environment and Learning: A Quantitative Synthesis," *Journal of Experimental Education* 50 (1982): 144–151.

17. Karl R. White, *The Relationship between Socioeconomic Status and Academic Achievement* (Unpublished dissertation, University of Colorado, 1976).

18. Roland S. Barth, "Home-based Reinforcement of School Behavior," *Review of Educational Research* 49 (1979): 436–458.

The Barth review concludes that showing parents how to reinforce their children's positive behaviors usually produces positive effects on behavior. Even so, the studies focused on changing short-term misbehavior rather than directly raising achievement scores, and long-term changes are more difficult to demonstrate. If the reinforcement ends or the child becomes satiated, moreover, misbehavior and indifference to school may resume.

In defense of such principles, it can be argued that positive classroom behaviors such as attentiveness can demonstrably be changed, and they obviously influence learning of individual learners and their classmates. If the chosen reinforcement no longer works, another form may be substituted. As they grow older, for example, children may be more influenced by free playtime and money than gumdrops and praise. Perhaps cooperation and competition may have increasingly beneficial effects.

The workplace encouragement of adults through incentives may be intuitive, circumstantial, and not easily described; it may depend heavily on the idiosyncrasies of particular managers and workers. Similarly, constructive parental and instructional management of students may vary enormously depending on the circumstances. Stated in the abstract, however, the key is to employ reinforcers, monitor their results, and sustain them if successful or modify them if not.

FAMILY CHOICE OF SCHOOLS

More broadly, how can schooling help parents to help their children's learning? Letting parents choose their children's schools is one of the best solutions to America's K–12 achievement problem. When parents select schools, they feel more pleased with the school, and their children achieve more than their traditional public school peers. Why? To raise and maintain their enrollments, choice schools must appeal to parents, and they tend to be welcoming and involve parents extensively. Traditional public schools seem to be unresponsive to their customers—parents, students, and society in general—much like large business monopolies that remain indifferent to their customers' preferences. Status quo, indirect suppliers (that is, district, state, and federal bureaucracies and powerful special interests including teachers unions) exert strong and unhelpful influences.

As Caroline Hoxby has argued,[19] moreover, a school that the parents of a particular family find appealing will be much more successful with their children than other schools with features that may appeal to other families. The appealing features of the schools may be the principal's charisma, the school spirit, curriculum strengths, high achievement test scores, and a host of other definable and indefinable factors. Since, as previously stated, students spend about 92 percent of their time outside school, and families account for about the same percentage of learning, school choice is crucial. If the school choice can increase the family's learning efficacy by 10 percent annually, it would produce a huge effect over the 12 years of schooling, roughly twice as much as school factors by themselves can yield.[20]

What is the evidence? To assess the effects of school choice, I recently synthesized all the available school choice research I could find including small- and large-scale studies of programs in economically advanced and developing countries. Many of the studies traced student progress over time, concerned very large samples, or both. Caroline Hoxby and Paul Peterson's exemplary studies of charter schools and vouchers, respectively, were randomized experiments comparing children lotteried in and out of oversubscribed

---

19. Caroline M. Hoxby, "If Families Matter Most, Where Do Schools Come In?" in *A Primer on America's Schools* Terry M. Moe, editor (Stanford, CA: Hoover Institution Press, 2001).

20. Since, as Hoxby pointed out, 10 percent of 90 percent is nearly twice as much as 50 percent of 10 percent, even assuming an improbable 50 percent increase in school effectiveness.

choice schools. The most extensive research, however, was conducted overseas where whole countries have partially or wholly embraced parent-choice schooling.

Table 3 reviews the overall findings of 16 possible effects of four types of choice on four educational outcomes. The evidence sustains every single one of the 16 possible choice effects, and the

TABLE 3
Sufficiency of Evidence for Positive Effects

Form of Choice/Outcome	Value-Added Over-Time Achievement Gains	Cost Efficiency	Parent Satisfaction, Citizens' Favorable Regard, or Both	Social Integration, Citizenship, or Both
Charter Schools	Conclusive	Conclusive	Conclusive	**Suggestive**
Vouchers	Conclusive	Conclusive	Conclusive	**Suggestive**
Private Schools	**Suggestive**	Conclusive	Conclusive	Conclusive
Geopolitical Choice Intensity	**Suggestive**	**Suggestive**	Conclusive	**Suggestive**

Note: Adapted from Walberg, 2008. Over-time studies typically involve two or more years of test scores. Geopolitical choice indexes the degree of choice in an area such as a city, state, or nation. Components of the indexes are typically percentages of students in independent, parochial, charter schools, and being schooled at home.

evidence is conclusive rather than suggestive for 11 possible effects (none of the evidence for the possible findings was negative or insufficient). These results were extremely unlikely to occur by statistical chance and are about as consistent as any in the social sciences. Of course, not every choice school outperforms comparable traditional public schools, but it seems clear that school choice generally works.[21]

Perhaps the most interesting results are the positive effects of "geopolitical choice" or private provision of schooling within a community, state, or nation: the greater the degree of privatization, that is, percentage of students in parochial, independent, and charter schools and being home schooled, the higher the average achievement of all students in the area. This finding may be attributable to the generally positive effect of competition for consumers.

Choice schools save money, that is, their per-student costs are lower than traditional public schools. On average, charter schools in the U.S. cost an estimated 80 percent of traditional public schools; private schools cost about 50 percent. (The much greater numbers of parochial schools and their small costs compensate for the much fewer relatively expensive boarding schools and elite independent schools in big cities.) A growing majority of citizens support choice schools, and parents in choice schools are more satisfied than parents whose children attend traditional public schools where authorities tend not to send their own children. Choice schools are, contrary to frequent criticism, more integrated racially and socioeconomically, and their students are more often voluntarily active in charities and student civic affairs.

---

21. Herbert J. Walberg, *School Choice: The Findings* (Washington, DC: Cato Institute, 2008). See this publication for additional explanation of the conclusions and the assumptions on which they rest. Much of the most rigorous research, often carried out in whole nations, took place in Sweden, Eastern Europe, and Latin America. With national systems of education, many of which financially support public, parochial, and independent schools, investigators in these countries have been able to carry out nationwide studies. By comparison, U.S. voucher programs are tiny and usually confined to a single city. U.S. public, independent, and parochial schools are usually difficult to compare because they employ different examinations.

School choice results are consistent with findings in the manu-facturing and service industries. Almost all studies reveal that private provision of goods and services yields higher quality, a wider variety of choices, more satisfied customers, and lower costs than the government provisioning. Thus, school choice findings align with these extensively documented conclusions, which have been the impetus behind increasing privatization of public services in many countries including the United States.

5

INCENTIVES

The Congressionally sponsored Equality of Educational Opportunity survey brought salience to students' beliefs.[1] Those who agreed that ability and luck are more important than hard work in school tended to achieve less than others. Previously, psychologists found that students who work hard, that is, defer immediate gratification to reach long-term goals, are more often able to learn more and get farther in life. To function most effectively, they must often voluntarily or with reinforcing encouragement persist in goal-directed behavior to reach valuable short- and long-term outcomes.

As Walter Mischel and his colleagues found, enduring differences in self-control can be observed in children as young as four. Some were able to delay gratification longer than others, which appeared to help them develop into higher achieving, more socially competent adolescents who could cope better with frustration and stress.[2]

Self-reported motivation and achievement tests are moderately correlated. In 40 studies, the mean correlation between

---

1. Ibid. Coleman and others, 1966.
2. Walter Mischel, Yuichi Shoda, and Monica I. Rodriguez, "Delay of Gratification in Children," *Science* 244 no. 4907 (26 May 1989): 933–938.

motivation and achievement was positive (.34).[3] But this doesn't indicate the direction of causality, nor does it indicate what might best be done to improve motivation and learning. It remains to be shown that enduring motivation can be inspired or inculcated, at least by educators. A better source of inferring causality and improving learning is randomized experimentation with alterable practices.

INCENTIVIZED CONDITIONS

In a randomized experiment with Chicago Public School students in grades three through eight, Steven Brown and I[4] gave randomly chosen classes special instructions to do as well as possible for the sake of themselves, their parents, and their teachers. The control group received conventional test instructions. Even with the mildly incentivized instructions, the experimental group scored higher (.30 standard deviations) than the control group. Another part of the research project, however, yielded for middle-class suburban students a small effect (only .11, which, nonetheless, brought the experimental group to the 55th percentile of the control group). This early study suggested that even weak incentives in test instructions can raise achievement somewhat but may be more efficacious with poor, urban students.

Another study, conducted about the same time, used actual monetary incentives and reached similar conclusions. Brooks-Cooper studied test motivation among low- and middle-income black, Hispanic, and white high school students in Chicago and New York City. Groups that were paid for correct answers to National Assessment of Educational Progress questions scored higher (.28 standard deviations) than unpaid control groups, although the

3. Margaret E. Uguroglu and Herbert J. Walberg, "Motivation and Achievement: A Quantitative Synthesis," *American Educational Research Journal* 16 (1979): 375–390.

4. Steven M. Brown and Herbert J. Walberg, "Motivational Effects on Test Scores of Elementary Students," *Journal of Educational Research* 86 (1993): 133–136.

effect was larger for low-income minorities than middle-income whites.[5]

John Bishop's review of similar studies confirms the power of incentives including the threat or reality of negative incentives. The threat of grade retention, for example, can serve as an incentive for greater effort and learning success, though intensive remediation may be necessary.[6] An example is Chicago's Summer Bridge program, which gave parents and failing students the choice of grade retention or passing a final examination in an intensive, academically focused summer course. Depending on the grade level and subject, grade-equivalent increases in reading and mathematics scores over the short summer session ranged from one-half to a full year. The gains were extraordinary, time-efficient, and cost-effective, and they were retained in subsequent school years. The program, moreover, most benefited the initially lowest achieving students.

TESTING INDIFFERENCE

The foregoing results are important for several reasons. They suggest that students, like adult workers, are influenced by incentives. More recent studies discussed below suggest that monetary incentives even for teachers can yield positive effects on student learning. The results, however, raise questions about the results of tests employed by the National Assessment of Educational Progress, state assessments required by the No Child Left Behind Act, and traditional commercial tests.

5. C. Brooks-Cooper, "The Effect of Financial Incentives on the Standardized Test Performance of High-school Students" (Ithaca, NY.: Cornell University Graduate School Masters Thesis, 1993).

6. John Bishop, "Drinking from the Fountain of Knowledge: Student Incentive to Study and Learn—Externalities, Information Problems and Peer Pressure" in *Handbook on Economics of Education*, Vol. 2, Eric Hanushek and Finis Welch, editors, (Amsterdam: North Holland, 2006), 909–944.

The content of these tests is often unrelated to specific topics that students study; and their performance on such tests ordinarily does not affect their grades, college, or job prospects. Indeed, many students know that neither they nor their teachers will even see how well they have done. Karmos and Karmos's survey of 6th- through 9th-grade students showed that 47 percent thought such tests were a waste of time, 22 percent saw no good reason to try to do well, and 21 percent said they did not try very hard.[7]

The National Assessment Governing Board (NAGB, 1990) characterized the National Assessment of Educational Progress (NAEP) "as a survey examination which by law cannot be reported for individual students and schools." For this reason, NAEP may not be taken seriously enough by students to enlist their best efforts. Because it is given with no incentives for good performance and no opportunity for prior study, NAEP may understate achievement.[8] If true, it would be a rare piece of good news about American K–12 schooling.

INCENTIVES AND ASSESSMENT

These problems suggest two solutions that may work well, as John Bishop and others advocate. As discussed below, educational standards, curricula, instruction, and testing should be brought into close alignment; and students should be rewarded for good test performance possibly including admission and scholarships to leading colleges and universities. Moreover, as argued here, immediate monetary incentives may work even better.

---

7. Andrew H. Karmos and Joan S. Karmos, "Attitudes toward Standardized Achievement Tests and their Relation to Achievement Test Performance," *Measurement and Evaluation in Counseling and Development* 12 (July 1984): 56–66.

8. National Assessment Governing Board Issues for the 1994–1996 NAEP (Washington, DC, 1991), 17.

These solutions may go a long way toward improving learning by extending learning time, much of which is otherwise wasted. Bishop, for example, concluded that public schools with high-achieving students averaged about 75 percent of their school time for actual instruction. For schools with low-achieving students, the figure was 51 percent. The lower figure is attributable to absences, lateness, inattention, classroom disruptions, and teachers being off task. Students in East Asia spend roughly twice the time of U.S. students in regular and tutoring schools, and in individual study outside school. They center their efforts, moreover, on attaining well-defined academic standards.[9]

From synthesis of research on American states and foreign countries,[10] Bishop derived the features of successful systems of assessment and incentives. Assessments must have real consequences for students such as grade progression, graduation, and monetary rewards. Achievement should rise to an external standard, not merely achieving more than students' schoolmates. Bishop also finds that assessments are more effective when they serve as end-of-course examinations and when multiple levels of proficiency, particularly high levels, are indicated.

SELF-ESTEEM

Pop psychology and many educators often refer to "self-esteem." The National Association of Self-Esteem espouses it as a cure for social and individual ills through daily "I love me" lessons. The usual assumption is that higher self-esteem leads to better performance, success with others, and other desirable outcomes. To be sure,

9. Susan J. Paik, Debbie Wang, and Herbert J. Walberg, "Timely Improvements to Learning," *Educational Horizons* 80 (Winter 2002): 69–71.

10. John Bishop, "Drinking from the Fountain of Knowledge: Student Incentive to Study and Learn—Externalities, Information Problems and Peer Pressure," in *Handbook on Economics of Education*, Vol. 2, Eric Hanushek and Finis Welch, editors (Amsterdam, 2006), 909–944.

those with high self-esteem may say they are more attractive, likable, skilled, and accomplished. But such generous assessments are typically self-reported, and objective measures usually discredit both the assessments and their claimed effects.[11]

People with common self-esteem fluctuations, moreover, may on a given day be in a good mood and therefore rate their self-esteem, character, accomplishments, and circumstances highly. Thus, the correlations of self-esteem with performance and other outcomes may be attributable to the temporary mood of the day rather than that self-esteem is the enduring primary causal factor.[12]

Promoting self-esteem rather than accomplishment may be counterproductive. Youngsters and adults with the highest self-esteem (Should they be called egotists?) may appear charming on first hearing about their traits and accomplishments. They may be encouraged to exaggerate; they may speak up in groups and criticize others; but this may be self-defeating and undermine their own and others' potential accomplishments.[13]

Programs to boost self-esteem have not been shown to improve academic performance. Six psychological experiments with fifth-graders, for example, showed that those praised for intelligence did less well than those praised for effort. When they fail, students praised for intelligence may doubt both their ability and the sincerity of those praising them. In the experiment, they showed poorer task persistence, enjoyment, and performance. Praised for effort, the control groups believed they could succeed with greater effort and therefore made use of it.[14]

---

11. Roy F. Baumeister, Jennifer D. Campbell, Joachim I. Krueger, and Kathleen D. Vohs, "Does High Self-Esteem Cause Better Performance, Interpersonal Success, Happiness, or Healthier Lifestyles?" *Psychological Science in the Public Interest* 4, no. 1 (May 2003): 1–44.

12. Judith Rich Harris, "Socialization, Personality Development, and the Child's Environment," *Developmental Psychology* 36, no. 6 (November 2000): 711–723.

13. Ibid. Baumeister and others.

14. Claudia M. Mueller and Carol S. Dweck, "Praise for Intelligence Can Undermine Children's Motivation and Performance," *Journal of Personality and Social Psychology* 75, no. 1 (1998): 33–52.

Intrinsic Motivation

If children fail to make a sufficient effort to complete their seatwork and homework, a behavioral psychologist might recommend the use of *extrinsic motivation*, that is, external performance incentives such as allowing the child free play, providing praise, and perhaps giving them increased allowances for the good grades that result.

Despite the practical and scientific value of the behavioral perspective, critics insist that the use of extrinsic motivation risks diminishing self esteem, verbally expressed interest in learning, or intrinsic motivation. They leave parents and educators with alternatives of waiting for the "teachable moment" or the right developmental stage, both of which lack pragmatic and scientific proof. Fortunately, their contentions have been directly examined, and a synthesis of 96 experimental studies showed no consistent tendency for incentives to diminish intrinsic motivation.[15]

Why should this be so? Echoed by William James, Aristotle said we become what we do. Using incentives to form habits may make it easier for learners to see the value of desired behavior that isn't reinforced beyond the incentive period. Children, for example, use forks even when no longer praised for it.

Large-Scale Incentive Programs

The Advanced Placement examinations are the only common nationwide assessments of high-school students based on rigorous, external, and objective course standards. They cover more than 37 college-level courses and are given to more than half a million students

---

15. Judy Cameron and W. David Pierce, "Reinforcement, Reward, and Intrinsic Motivation: A Meta-Analysis," *Review of Educational Research* 64, no. 3 (fall 1994): 363–423, http://www.amazon.com/Rewards-Intrinsic-Motivation-Resolving-Controversy/dp/0897896777/ref=si3_rdr_bb_product.

annually to earn course credits at over 2,500 colleges, allowing successful students to graduate early or take more advanced courses. The O'Donnell Foundation used these tests as the basis of the apparently first large-scale demonstration of monetary incentives for public school students—the Advanced Placement Incentive Program.[16]

The Dallas Independent School District, where the program took place, had lower test scores than other parts of Texas, with African-American and Hispanic students trailing even further behind academically. Starting in the 1990–91 school year, the Incentive Program paid students $100 for each Advanced Placement (AP) examination passing score in English, Calculus, Statistics, Computer Science, Biology, Chemistry, and Physics. The teachers participating in the program received a $2,500 stipend for AP training and $100 for each of their passing students.

In the nine participating Dallas schools the year before the program began, 41 students passed AP exams. When the program ended five years later, 521 students passed the selected AP exams. Two years after the program ended, 442 students passed, a more than eleven-fold increase from the beginning of the program.[17] In interviews, students, teachers, administrators, and college counselors revealed enthusiasm for the Incentive Program. They reported that even students who failed AP exams improved their study skills and learned the value of hard work to achieve high standards.

The program benefited students in other ways. Those who passed a number of exams improved their chances of merit scholarships and admissions at top colleges and, since they had already passed college-level courses, they could potentially graduate from college early, saving money for their families and for taxpayers.

---

16. Herbert J. Walberg, "Incentivized School Standards Work," *Education Week* no. 18 10 (November 4, 1998): 48.

17. The results were replicated in 40 Texas high schools by Clement Kirabo Jackson. See "Cash for Test Scores: The impact of the Texas Advanced Placement Incentive Program," *Education Next* (2008). Available at: http://works.bepress.com/c_kirabo_jackson/10.

As in other areas of life, incentives work in schools as exemplified by the Incentive Program. Perhaps students find sports exciting and academics boring because of the lack of incentives. Students may need more than social promotion and graduating for mere attendance. Though not all incentives are monetary, rational people require reasons to work hard. Even if such thinking is philosophically objectionable, educational incentives may be justified since in the form of raises, promotions, and perks, they shape much of adult work life, for which students are presumably preparing.

6

TEACHERS

Scholars in the fields of anthropology, economics, psychology, and sociology have taken an interest in teachers and how they are selected and retained. Anthropologists and sociologists have described how new teachers are often assigned to the most difficult schools for which they are ill prepared and why their initial experiences lead many to soon drop out of teaching.[1] For economists, teaching provides an excellent opportunity to study the supply and demand of labor. Psychologists have also been interested in the characteristics of teachers, particularly their pre-professional training, how they score on tests, their behavior, and how such things may affect their students' learning—the subjects of this chapter.

In the current public school system, a person can become a teacher by completing an education degree. They generally gain pay increases with additional years of experience and taking more education courses. Aside from the first two years of teaching experience, none of these are associated with student achievement gains.

---

1. See, for example, Willard Wallers's insightful ethnographic classic, *The Sociology of Teaching* (New York: Wiley, 1932). This work pioneered in what became the "Chicago school" of professional socialization, which often concerns the fit or lack of fit between what professional education imparts and what is required on the job.

In most other occupations, job security and pay are based on productive merit. But failing teachers earn as much as teachers who
excel in the classroom, and current pay policies give failing teachers
no reason to change. In fact, more productive teachers, because
their efforts are not rewarded, may resent it and leave teaching.
Teachers may have little or no monetary reason to use their best
energy in the classroom rather than in moonlighting, travel, or their
own families.

A national survey of 853 public school superintendents and
909 principals revealed a majority of school leaders (76 percent of
superintendents and 67 percent of principals) said they need more
power to reward outstanding teachers, and almost the same percentages said they need more autonomy to remove unsuccessful
teachers. Most of those surveyed (96 percent of superintendents
and 95 percent of principals) said easing the process of removing
bad teachers, even those with tenure, would be "somewhat" or
"very effective."[2]

Teacher Selection and Compensation

The current policies for certifying, hiring, and paying teachers are
only supported by flawed studies. Because studies fail to consider
previous student achievement and demographics, the apparent
connection between teacher experience and student achievement
may be attributable to senior teachers' transfers to pleasant, middle-
class schools that may achieve well regardless.[3]

---

2. Steve Farkas, Jean Johnson, Ann Duffett, Tony Foleno, and Patrick Foley, *Trying
to Stay Ahead of the Game: Superintendents and Principals Talk about School Leadership*
(New York: Public Agenda, 2001).

3. A review of some 150 studies, tracked down with considerable effort, concluded
that the majority were flawed by the lack of student achievement as the criterion,
disaggregated measurements at the teacher or school level, and statistical controls for
alternative hypotheses including teacher characteristics and student socioeconomic
status and prior achievement [Kate Walsh, *Teacher Certification Reconsidered: Stum-
bling for Quality* (Baltimore, MD.: The Abell Foundation, 2001)]. Sponsored by the
U.S. Department of Education's Office of Educational Research and Improvement,

Restricting the sample of studies to the most rigorous research reinforces the possible importance of verbal skills and college selectivity, and indicates that teacher experience and graduate education degrees have very slight or no effects. Experience and education are significantly positive factors in a few studies, but in others, they are significantly negative. Overall, it appears that certified teachers perform very little or no better than those who are uncertified.[4]

Teaching makes up much of total schooling costs, but research indicates that current policies for hiring, retaining, and compensating teachers have long been arbitrary and ineffective. Schools are unnecessarily excluding candidates who are as likely to teach as well as the certified teachers that states and districts favor. Teach for America showed that recent graduates of elite colleges who are knowledgeable in their subjects, with no experience and little pedagogical training, are highly regarded by principals and are able to better promote student achievement than other teachers.[5]

Valid Teacher Tests

To implement the actionable implications of the findings, the American Board for the Certification of Teacher Excellence

---

another review found 57 acceptable studies among more than 300. Even so, the review corroborated other reviews in concluding that the research base is thin but suggests the probable importance of subject matter knowledge. [Suzanne M. Wilson, Robert E. Floden, and Joan Ferrini-Mundy, *Teacher Preparation Research: Current Knowledge, Gaps, and Recommendations* (Seattle: University of Washington Center for the Study of Teaching and Policy, 2001).

4. Dan Goldhaber, "The Mystery of Good Teaching," *Education Next* (Spring 2002): 50–55. A few studies suggest that the experience of the first few years of teaching may confer some benefits on student learning and that highly experienced teachers may "burn out."

5. Wendy Kopp, "Ten Years of Teach for America" in *Tomorrow's Teachers*, Margaret C. Wang and Herbert J. Walberg, editors (Richmond, CA: McCutchan, 2001), 221–234 and Margaret Raymond and Stephen Fletcher, "Teach for America: The First Evidence on Classroom Performance," *Education Next* (Summer 2001): 62–70.

(ABCTE)[6] developed examinations of professional and subject matter knowledge and now offers the Passport to Teaching alternative teacher certification program, valid in seven states. The Passport to Teaching certifies teachers for elementary education (K–6), English/ language arts (6–12), mathematics (6–12), general science (6–12), biology (6–12), physics (6–12), chemistry (6–12), and special education (K–12).

The Passport to Teaching program is enlarging the number of desirable candidates for teaching positions. Nearly 3 in 10 college-educated, non-teaching adults said they would consider a teaching career except for the required year or two of education courses. A Tarrance Group poll of Florida residents discovered that 82 percent felt that "someone with several years of real-world experience in the subject they want to teach, who knows the strategies of excellent teaching but has never taught before," would make an effective teacher.[7]

The evidence supports the use of the new test to select teachers. A sample of Tennessee 4th- through 6th-grade teachers took the two ABCTE examinations needed for elementary certification: the Professional Teaching Knowledge exam and the Multiple Subject Exam. The teachers who passed the exams improved student achievement more than the teachers who failed.[8]

Mathematica Policy Research conducted an independent study of ABCTE Passport-certified teachers that revealed principals found these teachers as "effective" or "somewhat more than effective" than "all other teachers [they had] observed in their career."[9]

6. Disclosure: In the past, the author served as a board member and advisor for this organization.

7. Tarrance Group (2007) Unpublished survey, http://www.tarrance.com.

8. Josh Boots, "Student Achievement and ABCTE Passport to Teaching Certification in Elementary Education" (Paper presented at the 2007 American Educational Research Association national conference in Chicago, IL. Washington, DC: American Board for the Certification of Teaching Excellence).

9. Steven Glazerman and Clarence Tuttle, *An Evaluation of American Board Teacher Certification: Progress and Plan* (Washington, DC: Mathematica Policy Research, Inc., 2006). MPR Reference No. 6215–400.

This is the first report of a five-year longitudinal study of the Passport program, which includes students randomly assigned to Passport and other teachers to rigorously evaluate the program. (Similar results are unavailable for the Praxis test.)

ABCTE, of course, does not guarantee successful teachers, but ensures that beginners have the professional knowledge required for the job, specifically, knowledge of their subject and how to teach. Moreover, the research carried out thus far suggests that teachers who can demonstrate this knowledge achieve more with their students than those who cannot.

PERFORMANCE PAY

Many economists and behavioral psychologists believe that appropriate incentives raise performance, which automatic raises fail to do. Clearly, incentives aren't all monetary. Industrial psychologists include praise, the prestige of the organization, the satisfaction of a job well done, and appealing working conditions, as well as the desires for fair play, team spirit, and excellence. Firms try to use these motivators to improve performance.

Still, the primary motivator is pay. In private firms and federal agencies, research demonstrates that performance pay positively affects performance.[10] Over 75 percent of salaried employees in private firms receive pay based in part on performance,[11] and government agencies are moving to that system.[12] In fact, private firms are reducing the percentage of base pay and increasing the amount of

10. Edward P. Lazear and K. L. Shaw, *Personnel Economics* (Cambridge, MA: National Bureau of Economic Research, 2007).

11. Michael J. Podgursky and Matthew G. Springer, "Teacher Performance Pay," *Journal of Policy Analysis and Management* 26, no. 4 (2007), 909–949.

12. S. Nelson, "Performance-based Pay in the Federal Government," (Unpublished paper presented at the Vanderbilt University conference "Performance Incentives: Their Growing Impact on American K–12 Education," February 28, 2008).

performance pay. As the crisis continues in American schools, policy makers are considering and beginning to enact legislation for performance pay for K–12 educators.

Paying for Star Performance

A tiny number of musicians, artists, athletes, and actors earn millions of dollars a year in the competitive marketplace, while the majority may not even be able to earn a living in their chosen field. Who wants to listen to a local violinist when the world's best are readily available on CD? In competitive fields, especially when facilitated by technology, the market decides performance pay, and consumers and the famous few hugely profit. Consider an extreme example from Korea where education is taken perhaps as seriously as anywhere.

The highly competitive for-profit *hagwon* tutoring industry for elementary, high school, and other students earns $15 billion per year.[13] In 2000, the firm Megastudy began putting up Web-based education services and now offers 2,000 courses, where the instructor of each course is paid approximately one-quarter of the tuition fees. One charismatic English teacher earned $2 million in one year. (Educational technologists joke that future K–12 teachers will make seven-figure incomes—all ten of them.) This entrepreneurship and differential pay hardly exist in American public schools, which may be a reason for their poor and costly offerings and where performance and customer satisfaction count for little.

The economists Lazear and Shaw[14] point out that most of today's employees are driven to achieve more, and that some workers are monetarily and otherwise attracted to demanding but highly rewarded work. Aspiring doctors, lawyers, and MBAs expect a

13. Herbert J. Walberg, *School Choice: The Findings* (Washington, DC: Cato Institute, 2007).
14. Ibid. Lazear and Shaw.

demanding education followed by years of long, grueling work-weeks. Not everyone who begins persists, but those who do can earn several times more than the average worker. These and similar groups remain under pressure; professionals who do not serve their clients satisfactorily may lose them, and MBAs can be laid off when they or their firms falter.

Newspaper writers, automobile and railroad workers, public school teachers, and those in other heavily unionized industries have faced no such pressures. On the other hand, the very existence of their industries are threatened, and ultimately so too are their jobs.

LACK OF TEACHER INCENTIVES

Teachers take easy "Mickey Mouse" undergraduate and graduate courses, face little accountability on the job, and obtain secure tenure in a few years. Under union contracts, they are typically required to work six-hour days. While the usual worker puts in 220 8-hour days annually, teachers work 180 days.[15] Thus, teachers work less, or 61 percent (6/8*180/220) of the time of typical workers and much less than other professionals who may work 9- or 10-hour days.

Private firms require managers to rank their staff and often prohibit uniformly high rankings. Rewarding managers for their division's productivity gives them an incentive to performance-rank their staff. Because teachers dislike being compared and held accountable, principals are disinclined to rank them, but research reveals that principal rankings line up with teachers' effects on student progress.[16]

Education research, moreover, suggests that performance pay[17]

---

15. Ibid. Lazear and Shaw.
16. Ibid. Podgursky and Springer.
17. David Figlio and L. Kenny, "Individual Teacher Incentives and Student Performance," *Journal of Public Economics* 91, no. 5 (June 2007): 901–914.

increases student achievement and leads to recruitment and retention of better teachers.[18] Private school teachers receive bonuses up to 10 percent of their base pay, which may be one of the reasons why, despite tuition costs, many parents prefer private schools.

Thirty states enacted legislation enabling performance-based teacher pay,[19] but only 12 percent of U.S. school districts employ it, most often for obtaining credentials like the National Board for Professional Teaching Standards certification, which has been shown to be only weakly related to student achievement gains.[20] Even then, merit pay represents only 2 percent of a teacher's base salary.[21]

More than 70 percent of voters favor paying better teachers more than others and extra pay for hard-to-recruit teachers of mathematics and science, and for teaching in high-poverty schools. This voter support is leading to new performance-based compensation policies. As more people recognize that education degrees and teaching experience don't improve student achievement and, as methods for assessing teacher improve, the laws and policies may expand performance pay.

PAY FOR CONTRIBUTION

The growing evidence that performance pay helps recruit and retain better teachers led the National Governors Association Center for Best Practices to release a report—Hassel and Hassel's *Improving Teaching through Pay for Contribution*, which presents new policies

---

18. Robert Reichhardt, *MCREL Research Report: Recruiting and Retaining Teachers with Alternative Pay* (Aurora, CO: Mid Continent Research on Education and Learning, 2002).

19. Philip Gonring, Paul Teske, and Bradley Jupp, *Pay-for-performance Teacher Compensation: An Inside View of Denver's ProComp Plan* (Cambridge, MA: Harvard Education Press, 2007).

20. Dale Ballou and Michael Podgursky, *Teacher Pay And Teacher Quality* (Kalamazoo, MI: W.E. UpJohn Institute, 1997).

21. Ibid. Podgursky and Springer.

for teacher pay.[22] "Pay for Contribution" is a new phrase among education policy makers, meaning basing pay on student gains, the difficulty of staffing certain schools, rare or special skills, advanced subject matter degrees, and mentoring other teachers. A United Kingdom program gave productive teachers 15–22 percent higher pay, and found that those teachers advanced student learning by an average of half a year further than other teachers during a two-year period.[23]

While pay differentials of less than 5 percent might not justify the administrative or political price, they may help retain high performers in at least acknowledging them publicly. Hassel and Hassel point out that larger incentives can raise the percentages of high-performing teachers.

In performance-pay plans, bonuses apparently work better than salary increases, since salary increases allow resting on one's laurels. Bonuses can reward both individual and team efforts. Either way, Pay for Contribution, the Hassels argue, requires fair measures of performance, recognition of high average and outstanding performers, frequent feedback on progress, and emphasis on all important job objectives. They further argue that policy makers must incorporate fairness, transparency, validity, and breadth of applicability to make Pay for Contribution successful.

---

22. Bryan C. Hassel and Emily A. Hassel, *Improving Teaching Through Pay For Contribution* (Washington, DC: National Governors Association Center for Best Practices, 2007).

23. Described in Hassel and Hassel.

7

CLASSROOM PRACTICES

Rigorous research on the achievement effects of teaching and other classroom practices gathered momentum in the early 1960s. By 1970, the research mushroomed, and the need for synthesizing hundreds of studies became apparent. Specialists wrote critical reviews of the research intended for scholars in education and psychology. To make practical use of the findings, three large agencies began projects to synthesize the findings and asked me to help compress the findings for educators into research-based teaching principles. These included the U.S. Department of Education under the leadership of Secretary William Bennett and Assistant Secretary Chester Finn; the United Nations which serves educators in more than 100 countries; and the U.S. Navy, which is challenged to efficiently and quickly educate recruits and officers about new technical developments.[1] This chapter draws on the findings from these projects.

---

1. Though responsible for the summaries here, I recommend the original publications, which have much more information and references to research and practice. The UNESCO booklets can be accessed and downloaded at http://www.ibe.unesco.org/publications.htm for individual reading and free republication. The Navy's comprehensive report was published in a special issue of the *International Journal of Educational Research*, which, as editor, I invited them to write. See William E. Montague and Fred G. Knirk, "What Works in Adult Instruction: The Management, Design, and

TEACHING

Uniform standards and well-thought-out curriculum guides can help keep students in the same grade learning the same things even in different schools within a district, state, or possibly nation. Given such consistency, student migration from one school to another becomes less problematic, and teachers can confidently predict what students have previously been taught.

Given broad agreement on standards, teachers can set the goals, schedule, methods, and evaluation of lessons to use class time effectively and appropriately for their students.[2] Well-developed long-term and daily lesson plans help ensure coverage of the important topics, that instruction begins and ends on time, and that transitions between units and parts of lessons are smooth and logical. A variety of activities can stimulate interest.

Teaching overviews show students the purpose of each activity and how it is related to other activities. Pretests inform the teacher of what students already know, which avoids excessive re-teaching,

---

Delivery of Instruction." *International Journal of Education,* Special issue, vol. 19, no. 4 (1993): 329–443.

2. The authors and titles of the United Nations booklets are Jere Brophy, *Teaching*; Sam Redding, *Parents and Learning*; Herbert J. Walberg and Susan J. Paik, *Effective Educational Practices*, Douglas A. Grouws and Kristin J. Cebulla, *Improving Achievement in Mathematics*; Keith Topping, *Tutoring*; Elliot L. Judd, Lihua Tan, and Herbert J. Walberg, *Teaching Additional Languages*; Stella Vosniadou, *How Children Learn*; Sharon L. Foster, Patricia Brennan, Anthony Biglan, Linna Wang, and Saud Al-Ghaith, *Preventing Behavior Problems*; Inon I. Schenker and Jenny M. Nyienda, *Preventing HIV/AIDS in Schools*; Monique Boekaerts, *Motivation to Learn*; Marie J. Elias, *Academic and Social-Emotional Learning*; Elizabeth S. Pang, Angaluki Muaka, Elizabeth B. Bernhardt, and Michael L. Kamil, *Teaching Reading*; Trudy Wallace, Winnie E. Stariha, and Herbert J. Walberg, *Teaching Speaking, Listening, and Writing*; Chung-wai C. Shih and David E. Weekly, *Using New Media*; John Lybolt and Catherine Gottfred, *Promoting Pre-School Language*; John E. Mayer, *Creating a Safe and Welcoming School*. The booklets are available from the United Nations International Bureau of Education, Geneva, Switzerland, and also freely downloadable and republishable from the Internet site http://www.ibe.unesco.org/en/services/publications/educational-practices .html. Originally published in English, most of the booklets on the site have been translated into Chinese and Spanish; fewer are in other languages.

and signals students about what is important to learn. Students in well-managed classes know what is expected of them and stay on task, moving through material at optimum speed determined by the teacher's accurate assessment of what requires more and less time. Skilled teachers can set standards that challenge students without protecting them from temporary failure and without setting impossible goals.

Tables, charts, and diagrams can help explain related ideas, and difficult material is often best presented in small steps while explaining new subject matter to students. Knowledge and comprehension questions simultaneously involving old and new ideas are likely to engage students, and their answers reveal to the teacher their degree of understanding.

Teachers can deepen understanding by neither accepting nor rejecting answers quickly but encouraging students to defend their answers thoughtfully and unhurriedly. Temporarily suspending their own views, teachers can heighten engagement by allowing several students to voice alternative explanations. At some strategic point, of course, effective teachers make clear the best answer and its reasons, or concede that not all questions have such single best answers. Even then, they may explore with their students the planning of real or hypothetical means of providing better answers.

Teachers can exhibit the learning strategies they want their students to follow. In "think alouds," they can describe each step of a task as they do it, and remind students of each activity's purpose. To assess comprehension, they can ask students to think aloud in pairs, small groups, and before the whole class. Students can learn from one another when they do drills and perform experiments in pairs or small groups under a teacher's supervision.

Homework extends class time so students can practice, in applying a lesson's new and difficult ideas to different contexts, which promotes their broader understanding of complex subjects. To make the most of homework, teachers can grade it, comment on it, ask pairs of students to discuss their answers with one another, and carry out whole-group discussions of critical ideas.

"Direct instruction" or traditional teaching done well, is often the best choice for whole classes taught at the same time. It includes daily review and, if necessary, re-teaching; step-by-step presentation of new content (the more difficult the subject, the smaller the steps); classroom practice in the form of solicited oral responses, seatwork and board work; discussion, reinforcement, and corrective feedback; and homework that is commented upon or graded.

Direct instruction assumes the students need the same activities, but the content may be too challenging for some students while others may already know it. "Mastery learning" allows students to proceed at their own pace until they pass mastery tests. Since mastery learning is difficult to design and implement, technology, as discussed briefly below and in greater depth in a subsequent chapter, has much to offer.

Using New Media

New media including CDs, DVDs, and the Internet may revolutionize education by quickly, conveniently, and cheaply providing information and even individually tailored instruction. Selectivity is of course crucial and students should be protected from access to pornography, depicted violence, and copyright infringement. When the Internet is unavailable at school and at home, DVDs, CDs, and cheap reprinting of out-of-copyright material may serve.

Described in a subsequent chapter, SearchLit.org provides more than 15,000 freely downloadable, printable, re-publishable children's books selected for quality and classified by grade level, topic, and virtues such as courage and perseverance. A school district, for example, may download its chosen selection of say, 500 books, and equip each school and child with a library for leisure or curriculum-related reading on a CD with a unit cost of as little as 25 cents. Students, of course, may feel more at ease than adults in reading material from computer screens, but the material can also be printed.

Interrelated texts, graphics, and sounds distributed over the Internet may engage students more than readings alone. Voluminous, valuable material for teaching is already available from such organizations as Chicago's Museum of Science and Industry, the Louvre, and the National Aeronautics and Space Administration to engage and teach students.

TUTORING

One-on-one and small-group tutoring can strongly influence achievement by providing students with quick, individualized feedback. Under skilled tutors, students may learn how to correct themselves and measure their progress. When tutoring their classmates and younger students, they can benefit because they may have to organize the subject matter, prepare suitable lessons, and answer unanticipated questions. However, tutoring materials and protocols prepared by others can save preparation time (and, as a subsequent chapter illustrates, the tutoring burden can increasingly be shifted to computer technology which continues to grow cheaper and more effective).

Tutoring guidelines may be most helpful when focused on what to do rather than what not to do. Tutors can ask questions and allow students time to think before prompting a response. Tutors can explore with tutees not only correct answers but how to hypothesize and test their initial answers. Tutors can sincerely praise students for progress made, for example, when students go for longer periods without making mistakes, and when they catch their own mistakes and explain the reasons.

EFFICIENCY-DRIVEN ADULT EDUCATION

The military and business firms face challenges in training and educating a range of students from ill-prepared high school graduates to senior officers with graduate degrees. They aim to prepare staff with knowledge and skills that require specified standards of uniformity (as required, for example, by the federal No Child Left Behind legislation that the 50 states are now attempting to attain). Educators in large firms and the military often employ extensive resources to design, develop, and evaluate courses and programs that achieve high standards with cost- and time-efficiency. Efficiency derives from:

- Aligning instructional content and methods to clear, well-specified, and measurable outcome standards;

- Developing computer programs that adapt pacing to an individual learner's knowledge and abilities;

- Using recorded audio and animated, colored visuals along with text to present complex ideas and processes;

- Eliminating extraneous material that does not contribute to the attainment of the standards;

- Employing time-saving teaching protocols, methods, and increasingly, computer programs with embedded expertise that may only require routine staff administration to manage rather than deeply knowledgeable, skilled instructors; and

- Extending the use of well-tested material throughout the organization, reducing unit costs and standardizing end-knowledge and performance.

Though these features are increasingly prevalent, they are not, of course, present in all adult education.

The military and firms can often produce well-evaluated efficacy findings since, unlike K–12 educators and evaluators, they can randomly assign students to alternative methods in true experiments. In helping senior U.S. Navy education staff to compile such findings, I saw the potential value of sharing their work with primary, secondary, college, and other educators and invited them to contribute a special issue of the *International Journal of Education Research*,[3] which I edited at the time. The following summary of the Navy's compilation of such research begins with principles of instructional design and describes various means of presentation. The special character of multimedia technology is then explained before turning to the evaluation and management of instruction.

Course Design

What are the education needs, the course goals, and mastery standards? This question should guide the planning of courses. Specific goals encourage learners and facilitate measurement of their progress toward the goals. Course materials and instruction should, of course, primarily reflect course goals, but they should also reflect students' desires to satisfy their curiosity and acquire general knowledge, and to learn things that will advance their job-specific skills and their careers.

Strategic time use may be crucial, but attainment of mastery takes precedence over individual learning speeds. In other words, attempts should be made to bring all students to a specified level of proficiency even if the amounts of time learners require substantially vary. Long bouts of intense training may risk losing student interest, and courses are often more effective when sessions are shorter and spread over a longer period of time. For unavoidably long sessions, a variety of activities may be helpful in promoting attention. Since students forget the most shortly after learning, built-in refresher sessions may be necessary over longer time periods.

Job-related education should resemble future actual tasks as

---

3. William E. Montague and Fred G. Knirk, "What Works in Adult Instruction: The Management, Design, and Delivery of Instruction," *International Journal of Education*, Special issue, vol. 19, no. 4 (1993): 329–443.

closely as possible, and use the same or similar tools and operations that the tasks require. For field-experienced students, such reality simulation may be less necessary.

Presenting Courses

If courses are conventionally taught, instructors should be able to demonstrate knowledge mastery and facile execution of skills to exemplify what is desired and potentially to inspire students. Listening to students can help instructors connect material to what they already know and to suggest extra study as needed. Instructors should give feedback on homework and tests as soon as possible, and should usually give correctives or negative feedback cordially and, if possible, privately.

Homework provides more practice time, and it should be related to real-world tasks. Tests help people learn, and should be as work related as possible. Students need to practice with instructor supervision, encouragement, and feedback. Open-book tests and the use of maps and guides may work well for simulations that assume the presence of these materials.

Used in longer courses, peer-to-peer teaching requires students to learn unique content on their own, teach it to classmates, and to be similarly taught. This technique can encourage independent study, reciprocity and teamwork, and mutual coaching. "Jigsaw" variations of peer teaching require the combination of each team member's unique learning to solve a difficult problem presented to the team. Such experiences require skillful planning and monitoring.

Computers and Multimedia

Course designers may decide that computer technologies and multimedia efficiently propel mastery of course goals and should be employed. High preparation costs and substantial efforts may be worthwhile if such courses are widely used. Centrally designed by subject matter and instructional experts, such courses provide standardization and can be distributed to remote locations that lack such expertise.

Self-paced courses can save student and instructor time by a third. With an instructor available to give feedback, programmed training can be more effective than traditional classrooms, and better results from independent study can be expected as the technology improves.

New courses may be tried even during the design stage to reveal where adjustments are necessary and later to remove kinks and inefficiency before the course is made widely available. Programs may need updating, continuing evaluation, and student feedback to improve them so that they continue to meet required course goals and standards. Like conventional instruction, multimedia courses should present information in learnable segments, and require appropriate student responses before proceeding to the next segment.

Complex tasks take time to master, and computers give students that time and simulate real-life situations. In simulations, conceptual fidelity may be more important than physical fidelity; simplified graphics of physical parts, for example, may at first be more comprehensible than photos and actual parts introduced later. Videos showing motion may be particularly useful in showing such things as flows of information and evolution of systems. Interactive programming can allow students to explore the consequences of situational changes. Given student responses, they can provide reinforcement and corrective feedback. Internet and hypertext links can connect students with alternate explanations and illustrations depending on the student's progress and interest.

Managing Courses

Well-managed courses tend to initially excel and continue to improve. As in schools, skilled, fully engaged managers can observe, evaluate, and supervise instructors; their mid-course evaluations and feedback can improve the end results. Such managers can gather suggestions for revamping centrally or locally designed courses.

Managers can also positively affect the morale of the organizations within their purview. They may be able to provide places where students and instructors can talk about their coursework and where they can read course-related magazines and books. Perhaps needless to say, computer labs and classrooms should be neat, well lit, and comfortable.

THE ART OF TEACHING

Despite the findings about teaching practice described in this chapter, future research may uncover subtle insights that illuminate the art of teaching and point to the nuanced perceptions of great teachers. Two promising topics are perceptions great teachers have about their students' behavior and, based upon them, moment-to-moment lesson changes.

Psychologists, for example, demonstrated that youngsters and adults think with their hands. Some teachers can consciously or unconsciously detect from their students' hand movements their readiness to understand successive difficult points in mathematics lessons. In an interview, Susan Goldin-Meadow said,

> Gestures are concrete manifestations of ideas for all the world to see. . . . Gestures provide useful clues to teachers because they allow students to express new information without having to disrupt their existing method of communicating. . . . Gestures also help students express ideas before they have connected their thoughts with the appropriate vocabulary.[4]

---

4. Susan Goldin-Meadow and Mary A. Singer, "From Children's Hands to Adults' Ears: Gesture's Role in Teaching and Learning," *Developmental Psychology* 39, no. 3 (2003): 509–520.

Teachers may perceive other subtle but important physical clues. An example is the change in dilation of the pupil.[5] Increases in pupil size are produced by stimuli such as friendly laughing. Great teachers may consciously or unconsciously respond to such subtle student signals by continuing or changing what they are doing in the lesson. From observing students' behavior they may learn what works well in their teaching.

It may be a long while before such teaching clues are well understood, and they may be found to vary with students' age and background. The understanding of such clues may not, however, be enough; it may be difficult to impart such clues and skills in using them. For present purposes, these investigations indicate that there is still much to learn about the subtleties of teaching. In the meantime, the large corpus of research summarized in this chapter and the work cited provides guidelines for improving teaching, teacher education, and continuing professional education of experienced teachers.

---

5. Timo Partalaa and Veikko Surakka, "Pupil Size Variation as an Indication of Affective Processing," *International Journal of Human-Computer Studies* 59, nos. 1–2 (July 2003): 185–198.

8

SCHOOL POLICIES

Because of the quality of teaching and the students themselves, classes within a school can vary greatly in their capacity to advance achievement. Even so, the school as a whole may have psychological features that set it apart from other schools and that affect its overall influence on what students learn. Though the research basis of school-level findings are less rigorous than those on classroom practices, two topics—safe, welcoming schools and school leadership—are worth considering since they help set the stage for effective classroom practices.[1]

SAFE, WELCOMING SCHOOLS

Psychological studies suggest that good morale in firms and other organizations promotes productivity. Similarly, schools that are secure and friendly appear to be better than others in promoting

---

1. Derived from the United Nations booklets Sharon L. Foster, Patricia Brennan, Anthony Biglan, Linna Wang, and Saud Al-Ghaith, *Preventing Behavior Problems* and John E. Mayer, *Creating a Safe and Welcoming School*. Discussed earlier, the booklets are available from the United Nations International Bureau of Education, Geneva, Switzerland, and also freely downloadable and republishable from the Internet site http://www.ibe.unesco.org/en/services/publications/educational-practices.html.

learning. In various ways, schools can encourage students concern with the well-being of others and tolerance of views that differ from their own. Arriving to class on time, following school dress codes, and avoiding disruptions may reveal students' social maturity. To help establish these things, some schools issue handbooks with reasonable expectations and rules clearly set forth. Some psychologists believe that engaging students to develop and revise such handbooks makes them more effective.

School-related extracurricular activities and exhibiting student work may help students feel psychologically closer to their schools. Newsletters for parents may also encourage their presence and pride in the school. Teachers can send notes to them about the class's academic progress and ways that parents can help students learn. Teacher-parent conferences and social occasions can reinforce desired behavior through positive communication.

Many schools are plagued with behavior problems, including violence and illegal drugs. Though such problems are not educators' primary responsibility, they may be able to help prevent them at least on school grounds. Prevention might best start early, even though educators may have little influence at life's beginning. Even the mother's stress during pregnancy can affect the child's later well-being. In areas with high instances of crime and delinquency, schools, hospitals, and other community organizations offer parenting programs that can help children face decisions about their behavior starting even in preschool. Early intervention can lead to lower instances of smoking, illegal drug and alcohol use, sexual activity, and delinquency by the time children reach adolescence. Removing opportunities may also be helpful. Some schools must regrettably search students as they enter campus to detect weapons, alcohol, and drugs.

Parents and teachers can set good examples and thoughtfully and critically discuss television shows and movies that glamorize drugs and violence. Nominally in control of only 8 percent of the first 18 years of students' lives, regular schools in the end may have to remove incorrigible students in their efforts to fulfill their primary achievement mission.

School Leadership

The behaviors of effective principals cohere well with those of teachers as described in this book. Based on extensive research and field-testing, Goldring, Porter, Murphy, and others developed a conceptual framework and a set of indicators of effective school leadership that principals can employ.[2] According to their research, what distinguishes such leadership is the following:

- *High Standards for Student Learning*, meaning individual, team, and school goals for rigorous student academic and social learning;

- *Rigorous Curriculum* in the form of ambitious content provided to all students in core academic subjects;

- *Quality Instruction*, or effective instructional practices that maximize student academic learning;

- *Culture of Learning and Professional Behavior*, that is, communities of professional practice in the service of student academic and social learning and a healthy school environment in which student learning is the central focus;

- *Connections to External Communities*, or linkages to family and other people and institutions in the community that advance academic learning;

- *Performance Accountability* in the form of leadership holding everyone responsible for realizing high standards of performance for student learning; and

2. Ellen Goldring, Andrew C. Porter, and Joseph Murphy, *Assessment Learning-Centered Leadership: Connections To Research, On Professional Standards, And Current Practice* (New York: Wallace Foundation, 2007).

- *Individual and Collective Responsibility for Learning* among both students and staff.

The findings in this chapter are less rigorously research-supported than many of the findings discussed in the previous chapters. Still, the leadership findings here cohere well with those in other chapters on the important role of parents in learning, standards and goals, effective teaching practices, and testing. The findings on safe, welcoming schools accord well with common sense; dangerous, unfriendly schools can hardly be expected to be effective in advancing achievement.

9

NEW TECHNOLOGIES

This chapter describes a sample of efficient computer, Internet, and social technologies that yield results equal to or better than conventional methods, often at a fraction of the usual monetary and time costs. They were selected on the basis of variety, research available, my personal experience seeing several in action, and being illustrative of how psychological principles can be automated and efficient. Other technologies that might have been chosen may be equal or superior to those mentioned here in advancing achievement.

COMPUTER AND INTERNET TECHNOLOGY

Together with the Internet, computers have greatly increased the efficiency of manufacturing, services, and our personal lives. E-mail, for example, is cheaper, faster, and more convenient than first-class and express mail. Automatic paycheck deposits and mortgage deductions, cash dispensers, and personal banking at home make most trips to the bank unnecessary. Amazon supplies nearly 200,000 different books for Internet downloading to Kindle, its new wireless reading device. Though a large bookstore might provide

100,000 titles, Amazon can provide next-day delivery for more than one million books. An estimated 1.3 million people make a living buying and selling objects of their interest on eBay. These and other technologies are also becoming cheaper and easier to use.

By comparison, the schools have been slow to take advantage of new technologies. But some exciting precedents can be described that have the potential to vastly and efficiently advance achievement.

Value-Added Accountability and Research

High achievement status of a school at a single point in time is likely to be misleading about the school's effectiveness. Schools with high achievement status do not necessarily make good achievement gains. As emphasized in previous chapters, family background is a powerful determinant of test scores. Students in affluent communities are likely to be ahead of others even before they start school and to achieve well even if their schools are ineffective. Some schools in poverty areas, moreover, make excellent gains, but at a given time their achievement status may be below average. For this reason, policy makers are turning to the year-to-year gains or value-added scores rather than achievement status at a single point in time as a better indicator of school success. Data systems (or "warehouses") of test scores and computerized statistical calculations enable states to more fully and fairly evaluate schools.

Tennessee has been the pioneer in this effort, and may be a decade ahead of other states. Though data for schools are often publicly available, the Education Consumers Foundation displays the school comparisons on the Internet and distributes comprehensible reports that compare schools to others in the same areas and to the averages of the state as a whole. These reports received much press attention and public interest, and members of several school boards previously thought successful as indicated by their status are being replaced.

Such data and analyses also allow practical research on the features of highly successful schools that may deserve imitation. Stone, Bruce, and Hursh's recent report[1] describes a dozen practices used in common by six of Tennessee's top-performing elementary and middle schools (see Table 4) out of over 700 statewide. Derived from such atypical cases, these findings corroborate other evidence described in this book including a strong focus on clear goals, sustained and engaged effort, close monitoring of results, constructive learning environments, and close contact with families.

Distance Education

Instructional technology is likely to prove more effective, cost efficient, and time saving than regular classroom teaching. In the most extensive synthesis of past research covering 232 control-group studies, Bernard and his colleagues found that student achievement, attitude, and retention were roughly the same for traditional classrooms and distance education. Distance education, however, can be delivered cheaply to hundreds of thousands of students by television and increasingly over the Internet.[2] Like computer programs, great care can be taken to design and evaluate distance programs. Teams of top subject matter experts, instructional designers, and teachers can bring their best to course design, much more so than any given single educator working alone.

Moreover, improvements in distance education can be expected. Computers and the Internet are increasingly faster and accessible. Unlike whole-class teaching, distance programs can be designed to adapt to students' individual abilities, interests, and

---

1. John E. Stone, Guy S. Bruce, and Dan Hursh, *Effective Schools, Common Practices* (Education Consumers Foundation, 2007), www.education-consumers.org/tnproject/practices.htm.

2. Robert M. Bernard, Philip C. Abrami, and Yiping Lou, "How Does Distance Education Compare with Classroom Instruction? A Meta-Analysis of the Empirical Literature," *Review of Educational Research* 74, no. 3 (Fall 2004): 379–439.

TABLE 4
Effective Schools, Common Practices

1. Use progress tests that assess the same skills that are tested on the state's Comprehensive Assessment Program (CAP) examinations.
2. Require students to meet higher-than-minimum mastery criteria on student progress tests.
3. Employ practice-intensive learning activities that target the types of skills required by the examination.
4. Provide principals with frequent reports of individual student progress with respect to the attainment of Tennessee's curriculum standards.
5. Provide teachers with frequent reports on the progress of each of their students.
6. Adjust teaching practices when a student makes insufficient progress toward a curricular objective. (Students simply are not permitted to quietly fail.)
7. Use student progress data to assess each teacher's classroom effectiveness. (Teaching performance is tracked continuously by the principal or by colleagues who are assigned to monitor teacher and student progress.)
8. Routinely work with struggling staff to improve their teaching skills.
9. Obtain for principals supplemental budgetary support for the training and materials required to improve teacher performance.
10. Regularly inform parents about their child's performance and seek to work with parents whenever children are progressing insufficiently.
11. Survey parents at least annually to assess satisfaction with the school's services.
12. Provide school-wide programs that reward positive social and academic student behavior. (Principals monitor the success of these programs, collecting data on the number and type of student referrals for problem behavior.)

Adapted from John E. Stone, Guy S. Bruce, and Dan Hursh (2007), *Effective Schools, Common Practices*. Education Consumers Foundation, www.education-consumers.org/tnproject/practices.htm.

circumstances. Although programs may be costly to design and build, once improved and field-tested to ensure high quality, they can be used with thousands of schools and homes at increasingly lower costs per student. "Winner-take-all" teachers or one-in-a-thousand top performers can record their presentations. Customized coaching and small-group discussions can proceed with e-mail, "texting," and other interactive systems.

Distance programs arose from non-distance, computer-based technologies for which control-group studies showed clear superiority over regular classroom instruction in eight (meta-analytic) reviews. Students in computer-based groups not only learned more on average but found their classes more enjoyable. Computer-based tutoring and acceleration classes for gifted students were especially effective.[3] As distance technology improves, greater effectiveness and efficiency can be expected, to say nothing of the convenience of access any time, any place.

Distance Testing

The federal No Child Left Behind legislation requires testing to measure how well schools are meeting state standards. In a perfect world, Adequate Yearly Progress (AYP) would be continuously measured, but that is currently impossible. With computer-administered tests, however, students can be periodically assessed throughout the school year. The not-for-profit Northwest Evaluation Association (NWEA), a consortium of school districts, has developed a reliable computer-administered assessment now used several times during the school year in approximately 6,000 schools around the country.[4] The NWEA tests are adaptive and give more

---

3. James A. Kulik, *Effectiveness of Instructional Technology in Elementary and Secondary Schools: What does the Research Say?* (Ann Arbor, MI: University of Michigan, 2001).

4. This subsection on distance testing is adapted from several paragraphs in Herbert J. Walberg, "Assessing Learning" in *Reforming Education in Arkansas* (Stanford, CA: Hoover Institution Press, 2005).

difficult questions to students who answer correctly and easier items to students who give incorrect answers so as to converge quickly and reliably on their achievement level and cut testing time by as much as 50 percent.

Computer-based tests can be calibrated to state achievement standards and can predict the likelihood of making AYP. As soon as they finish the test, students' scores are available. Detailed reports of each grade's performance can be produced within 24 hours, and reported in NCLB categories. Students can take the NWEA tests up to four times a year, often at a lower cost than paper-and-pencil tests, which are usually given only annually. NWEA tests produce scores comparable across grades, and therefore can be used to measure value-added progress. They can measure student progress across classes and schools, regardless of starting points.

Principals, teachers, and parents can use detailed NWEA reports the way firms use more frequent progress reports to guide ongoing decision-making. Reports can be presented to parents, school boards, and lawmakers in September, December, February, and May, for example. Rather than going to the expense, difficulties, and scandals of creating their own tests, some states are considering adopting the NWEA tests.

Headsprout Reading

It may be hard for adults to remember the difficulties of learning to read. How many need to be reminded that children need to know left from right to be able to distinguish the letters *b* and *d*? Can they remember all the time, patience, and tedium of those who instructed, encouraged, and corrected them in such minutia? If well defined, however, such teaching can be automated. With color, sound, and animation, it can be made enjoyable.

Headsprout Reading Basics, available to parents and schools, does just this. It establishes over the Internet the skills essential for reading success among nonreaders and beginning readers.[5] At a cost of $100, students learn letters, their sounds, and how the sounds are blended. As they advance through the lessons presented in accordance with their individual needs and progress, they learn to read words and sentences in simple short stories—in no more than 15 hours of typically 20-minute lessons. School districts are investing in the program to teach first through third graders who have not yet learned to read.

The program includes simple comprehension exercises to ensure reading with understanding. Students are required, for example, to identify correctly one of three pictures based on a sentence just read. If they respond incorrectly, the program recycles them through that part of the lesson or to another lesson until they acquire mastery of each skill.

Headsprout Independence builds on this foundation to provide mastery of additional sounds and word-deciphering strategies to extend the reading vocabulary to over 5,000 words. Children respond to longer and more complex passages until they reach the point of correctly completing exercises typical of standardized reading tests.

Developed by reading experts and behavioral psychologists, Headsprout employed a trial-and-error engineering approach informed by learning scientists and experienced educators. Like the Wright brothers, who made small changes in wing design until they got things right for the maiden flight at Kitty Hawk, the Headsprout

---

5. Joseph Layng, Janet S. Twyman, and Gregory Stikeleather, "Headsprout Early Reading™: Reliably Teaching Children to Read," *Behavioral Technology Today* 3, (2003): 7–20; and Janet S. Twyman, Joseph Layng, Gregg Stikeleather, and K. A. Hobbins (in press), "A Non-linear Approach to Curriculum Design: The Role of Behavior Analysis in Building an Effective Reading Program" in *Focus on Behavior Analysis in Education*, Vol. 3, W. L. Heward et al, editors (Upper Saddle River, NJ: Merrill/Prentice Hall). See also www.headsprout.com.

developers utilized the capacity to quickly change program features and measure their effects. Billions of children's electronically tabulated responses helped efficiently tweak the program.

On the surface the program appears to the child as an interactive cartoon. Underneath is a patented technology that systematically teaches the phonics skills to sound out words and begin reading with understanding. The program was so rigorously developed and tested that Headsprout offers schools a full product refund for each kindergarten or first-grade student who is not at or above grade level in the first grade.

The keys to the Headsprout success are:

- A complete and detailed specification of the pre-reading skills, such as individual letter recognition, that children need to become effective beginning readers;

- The precise recording of each child's responses so that reinforcements and correctives can be individually administered over the Internet with the patience, speed, and appropriateness that could not be achieved by a skilled tutor; and

- Continuous revision of the program based on children's responses.

Skilled reading is perhaps the most foundational of all academic skills. It is a difficult skill unattained by many high-school students and adults. Yet, the teaching of reading can be automated and provided at minimum cost. Though many third graders have yet to learn to read, the cost of their schooling is roughly $30,000 at a current cost of $10,000 a year. Headsprout guarantees success with 15 hours at 0.3 percent of the cost. Since beginning reading is difficult to teach, even greater success may be expected in mathematics and other subjects. Still new competitors seem bound to arise, which may challenge Headsprout and spur new and improved instructional offerings.

Social Technology

New forms of charitable organization enable people, both donors and recipients, to contribute to projects that would have little hope of achieving well on their own. Though computers and the Internet can facilitate such projects, the creative part is how they organize institutions and volunteers to efficiently provide opportunities.

Room to Read

On a Nepal trekking vacation from Microsoft in 1998, John Wood accepted an offer to visit a school.[6] He learned the library holdings consisted of *Finnegan's Wake*, a romance novel, and a travel guide to Mongolia—all kept under lock and key for fear the children would damage them. Wood collected over 3,000 books from friends, acquaintances, and donors and brought them back on six donkeys. In 2000, he devoted himself to the (nonprofit) Room to Read, which helped build more than 8,000 libraries in Nepal, India, Vietnam, Cambodia, Laos, and Sri Lanka and provided 2 million books, including books written by children in their native language. This number of libraries eclipses the numbers sponsored by one of America's greatest philanthropists, Andrew Carnegie, whose foundation built approximately 3,500 libraries, mostly in the United States.

Room to Read financially collaborates with local communities to give scholarships for girls and to build schools and computer laboratories, although it concentrates on building libraries. Grant recipients must put up a fraction of the cost of the library and form a board for its governance. Donors can specify what part of the program and what country their contribution funds.

Expanding faster than highly successful for-profits (including

---

6. See the Room to Read website http://www.roomtoread.org/about/index.html and Wood's book *Leaving Microsoft to Change the World: An Entrepreneur's Odyssey to Educate the World's Children* (New York: Collins, 2006).

Starbucks during its growth period), Room to Read is now in South Africa and Zambia and plans to be operating 10,000 libraries in 15 countries in Africa and Asia by 2010. My evaluation of Room to Read with Susan Paik showed that teachers and parents in the four beginning countries viewed their Room to Read libraries very favorably.[7]

Wikipedia

Both old and young academic fuddy-duddies may be quick to dismiss recently born *Wikipedia* because its content is nearly all consumer supplied and edited. Anyone at any time can submit or edit parts or all of an article (although many are screened by voluntary "super editors" who monitor articles within their specialty to guard against error, bias, and vandalism).

Wikipedia is free, nearly instantaneous in answering queries and is usually first- or near first-cited in objective Google searches. It contains more than 2.8 million articles in English alone, over 25 times more than the 240-year-old *Encyclopedia Britannica*. In response to current events and research, *Wikipedia* is updated daily. Perhaps along with *Science,* the most prestigious of all "hard" science journals, *Nature* reported that in 42 randomly selected general science articles, there were 162 expert-identified mistakes in *Wikipedia* versus 123 in *Britannica*.[8]

As its editors declare, *Wikipedia* requires expansion and improvement. With 25 times the number of articles and 76 percent of the accuracy of *Britannica* however, *Wikipedia* is only a few years old in contrast to the much older *Britannica*. At its current growth rate, *Wikipedia* seems likely to excel in quality as well as its astonishing size.

---

7. Susan Paik and Herbert J. Walberg, *Overview of the Room to Read Evaluation 2005,* http://www.roomtoread.org/programs/downloads/Monitoring_and_Evaluation_Summary.pdf.

8. "Internet Encyclopedias Go Head To Head," *Nature* (2006): 438, 8. 900–901.

SearchLit

The nonprofit website SearchLit[9] provides for free viewing, down-loading, and reproduction or republication of more than 15,000 outstanding, out-of-copyright, children's stories, poems, and books such as Louisa May Alcott's *Little Women*, Mark Twain's *Huckle-berry Finn*, and Stephen Crane's *Red Badge of Courage*. The books are computer analyzed to supply precision grade-level difficulty estimates. They have been categorized in various ways including virtues such as honesty, courage, and perseverance to facilitate reading choices by educators, parents, mentors, tutors, and children themselves. Also available are user-contributed lesson plans and many plays, poems, and stories as well as links to dictionaries, histories, world cultures, historical time lines, and children's book of the year awards from Australia, Britain, Canada, New Zealand, and the United States.

Why haven't schools made better use of psychologically valid practices described in previous chapters and the more efficient innovations in distance and social technologies described in this chapter? Despite substantially rising costs, why have schools made so little progress? These are questions to which the last chapter now turns.

---

9. See the site at www.searchlit.org.

10

CREATIVE DESTRUCTION

As discussed in the introduction, the first of the international achievement surveys published in the early 1960s showed American schools lagging behind those of other countries. Since then, evidence has accumulated showing a lack of substantial progress despite the world's highest or near highest per-student spending. Even with substantial and steady increases in funding and many reforms, schools have made little progress.

In "The Educational Quality Imperative," Eric Hanushek[1] shows that poor K–12 achievement threatens America's future, particularly for youth as they face the challenge of global competition for knowledge and skills. In contrast to the views of public educators, American students themselves believe they are insufficiently challenged. Citizens, too, are dismayed with the standards and offerings of the nation's public schools, and they favor radical reforms that have been slow in coming.

It is no longer a mystery how to advance achievement. The practices described in the preceding chapters include:

- High, uniform standards;
- Supportive school policies;

---

1. In preparation.

- Clear, measurable goals;

- Efficient means for achieving the goals;

- Opportunities for sustained, engaged student effort;

- Frequent, close monitoring of results;

- Appropriate reinforcement and correctives;

- Periodic, informative reports for parents, citizens, school boards, and legislators about achievement progress.

The problem is that the responsible parties—legislators, state and local school boards, and public school educators—failed to institute such reasonable policies and practices. Nor have they selected, employed, and evaluated the new computer, Internet, and social technologies of the kind described in the previous chapter that help to make education more efficient.

What is the solution? "Creative destruction" brought about by vastly increased school choice, particularly by private providers, including for-profit firms that, unlike large public bureaucracies, have strong incentives to meet performance standards and satisfy their customers.

What is creative destruction? Though he had predecessors, Joseph Schumpeter originated the term in 1942 and popularized it in the early 1940s as the transformative factor of technology in social and economic change. Unlike historians who described "great men" and wars, unlike sociologists who emphasized changes in social organization, and unlike economists of the time who pointed to changes in capital and labor, Schumpeter emphasized entrepreneurs who employ radical new technologies that are substantially more effective, efficient, or appealing than past and current technologies. In promoting progress, they eventually destroy older technologies, often employed by large established firms wedded to old ways.[2] As a result, firms and even whole industries may decline and fall.

These technologies may entail new products, services, and forms of organization, management, transportation, advertising, and financing. Muskets, for example, replaced long bows; plastic replaced glass and wood; and mini-mills replaced large steel mills. Now the Internet is replacing traditional publishing; digital is replacing film photography; television, cable, DVDs, and downloadable media are replacing theaters; mobile cell phones are replacing pay phones and even hard-wired home phones. Today, Google and other technologies challenge newspapers, book publishing, music distribution, and now even the cell phone industry.

Academics continue to study these technological revolutions. At the Harvard Business School, Clayton Christensen revived such thinking about industries in general and argued that "disruptive technologies" seem likely to transform schools.[3] At Stanford University, Paul Romer is the primary developer of New Growth Theory, which puts more emphasis on the force of new ideas than economists' traditional emphasis on additional labor and capital. Holding appointments at both institutions, Niall Ferguson explains in his world history of finance[4] how firms and financial systems were subject to mass extinctions like the many species subject to Darwinian evolution. The bank panics of the 1930s, the savings and loans failures of the 1980s, and perhaps today's mortgage meltdown are modern cases in point.

Given the school failures of the last half-century, the substantial progress needed undoubtedly requires more radical reforms

2. Joseph A. Schumpeter. *Capitalism, Socialism, and Democracy* (New York: Harper, 1975) [orig. pub. 1942].

3. Clayton M. Christensen, "Disruptive Innovation for Social Change," *Harvard Business Review* (December 2006); Clayton M. Christensen and Michael B. Horn, "How Do We Transform Our Schools?" *Education Next* 8, no. 3, (Summer 2008): 13–19.

4. Niall Ferguson, *The Ascent of Money: A Financial History of the World* (New York: Penguin Group, 2008).

than those of the past, specifically the more systematic enactment of well-evidenced technologies of the kind described in previous chapters. More than this, new forms of school organization seem most likely to provide the management and incentives to make use of successful technologies.

New K–12 Schooling Organizations

The previous chapter described examples of the kinds of technologies that might be employed, but equally important are new organizations that can assemble, invent, evaluate, improve, and integrate such components into a successfully functioning system of educational delivery. In "A New Era for America's Schools," for example, John Chubb and Terry Moe describe innovative organizations geared to the new technologies.[5] One example of their impressive evidence is the demand and rapid growth of virtual charter schools that provide distance delivery of education through the Internet. They serve 187,000 students in 24 state-level virtual schools including 62,000 in the Utah Electronic High School and 54,000 in Florida's Virtual School.

These virtual schools exemplify two requirements of the needed creative destruction—new technology and school choice. The positive effects of various forms of choice are described in Chapter 4. They echo the results of dozens of studies[6] of privatization of public services including police and fire protection, airlines, toll-way operation, road maintenance, and other services, which generally show better outcomes than public provision, lower costs, and greater satisfaction of employees and clients. Firms typically compete for contracts for such services. If they fail to meet performance specifications, they risk losing their contracts and even

---

5. Terry M. Moe and John E. Chubb, *Liberating Learning: Technology, Politics, and the Future of American Education* (San Francisco: Jossey-Bass, 2009).

6. Charles C. Wolf, *Markets or Governments: Choosing between Imperfect Alternatives* (Cambridge: MIT Press, 1988).

going out of business. The competitive effects and destruction of poor performers tends to quickly raise the bar.

Despite such industry precedents and the generally positive results of school choice programs, John Merrifield points out that the U.S. potential of school choice and privatization appears to be vastly underestimated.[7] Most of the nation's charter schools, for example, are small and individually governed by inexperienced boards unlikely to master complex government regulations, building acquisition and maintenance, labor relations, and the like— much less the integration of new technologies.

Private and charter schools and their boards may also be too small to attain the economies of scale, that is, to produce equal (or better) outcomes at reduced per-student costs as they grow larger, which would enable them to invest in research and development to improve their offerings. Even if successful, the small number of choice schools may be insufficient to produce strong, competitive, even creatively destructive effects on surrounding lackluster schools. Nonprofit private and charter schools, moreover, lack strong monetary incentives to raise achievement outcomes, reduce costs, offer distinctive goals and means, and to generally increase their appeal to their customers—parents and students.[8] As in other industries, for-profit colleges successful in these ways attract more students, increase their income, and can reward their shareholders, managers, and staff. They are rapidly growing.

Thus, although better practices described in previous chapters can improve achievement in conventional schools, market-based, consumer-driven school choice seems the best hope for creative destruction by new technologies. America's high technology and

---

7. On the prospects of bolder initiatives than those of the past, see *The Future of Educational Entrepreneurship: Possibilities for School Reform* Frederick M. Hess, editor (Cambridge: Harvard Education Press, 2008).

8. John Merrifield, *"The Dismal Science: The Shortcomings of US School Choice Research and How to Address Them."* Policy Analysis number 616 (Washington, DC: Cato Institute, April 2008).

free markets may bode well for such a combination, but can an affluent country in the West be named that shows the success that a fully-fledged, large-scale parental-choice system allows?

The Swedish Example

How can the most promising ways of improving K–12 education—school choice and technology—best be fostered? The answer appears to be freer markets and competition among schools. Consider the bold Swedish innovation. Perhaps more than those in other western European countries, Swedish authorities and citizens had been concerned about primary and secondary students' poor showing on international achievement surveys and the possible long-term consequences.[9]

In 1993, the Swedish government required all local education authorities to fund privately operated choice schools at a per-student cost close to that of nearby traditional public schools within their districts. New schools had to meet basic requirements including an open-admission policy under which schools had to admit all applicants regardless of ability, ethnicity, and socioeconomic level. The new policy did not rule out for-profit schools that conformed to the national policy.

Unlike the few small-scale, heavily regulated voucher plans in the United States, new voucher schools were established in a broad cross-section of neighborhoods, including high-income areas as well as locales serving predominately working-class and immigrant populations. In terms of scale, the number of independent schools saw a fivefold increase. Contrary to anticipated fears, neither economic segregation nor isolation of special-needs students grew. The new policy led to increased competitiveness, improved student

---

9. Some observations reported in this last section are based on conversations over about a decade with Swedish scholars and education ministry officials about education policy.

achievement, and greater parental satisfaction with their children's schools.[10]

Unexpectedly, for-profit chains of schools were founded and grew quickly. Ten chains have more than 6 schools, and 5 run more than 10 schools each.[11] With 30 campuses, the biggest for-profit is Kunskapsporten ("Knowledge Schools"), which the *Economist* describes as follows:

> Like IKEA, a giant furniture-maker, Kunskapsporten gets its customers to do much of the work themselves. . . . Youngsters spend 15 minutes each week with a tutor, reviewing the past week's progress and agreeing on goals and a timetable for the next one. This will include classes and lectures, but also a great deal of independent or small-group study. The Kunskapsporten allows each student to work at his own level and spend less or more time on each subject, depending on his strengths and weakness. Each subject is divided into 35 steps. Students who reach step 25 advance with a pass; those who reach steps 30 and 35 gain, respectively, a merit or distinction.

On a password-protected Internet site for each of the students and their families, Kunskapsporten reports the weekly progress in each course of study, which parents can review. By the time they finish, only a few students are unable to set achievement goals and attain them largely on their own, which should be expected of schooled adults. Kunskapsporten keeps quantitative records to determine which teachers do best as tutors or as subject matter teachers; tracking enables leaders to help or reassign laggards. Highly successful teachers receive bonuses, as do those who transfer from successful to unsuccessful schools. From annual payments of $8,000–$12,000 per student, Kunskapsporten makes an average return on capital of

---

10. F. Mikael Sandstrom and Fredrik Bergstrom, "School Vouchers in Practice: Competition Won't Hurt You!" *Journal of Public Economics* 89, nos. 2–3 (2005): 351–80.

11. "The Swedish Model," *Economist* (June 12, 2008): pp. 45–46. http://web.econ omist.com/displaystory.cfm?story_id = 11535645.

around 6 percent and is negotiating with U.K. authorities to open
schools in London.

Thus, Kunskapsporten and other Swedish for-profit school
firms show they can compete and thrive. Given monetary incentives, they can improve achievement, satisfy parents and students,
and quickly attract new customers. Kunskapsporten does so by
employing a system of variations of the successful practices
described in previous chapters including the kind of new technologies illustrated in the previous chapter. These include close working
relations with parents, regular Internet reports on their children's
progress, clear measurable goals, close computer monitoring of
achievement, student goal and time budgeting with a tutor's guidance, student (and teacher) incentives, and lesson pacing suited to
the learner's individual needs.

Why did this high-tech firm and other for-profit companies
pioneer and thrive with nationwide vouchers in Social Democratic,
"Old World" Sweden rather than in market-driven, capitalistic,
"tech-savvy" America?

CONCLUSION

American students are not learning nearly as much as they can, nor
as much as the competitive global economy requires. As exemplified in rigorous studies described in this book, the use of psychological principles can vastly quicken learning. Like biological principles
that underlie medical practice, these principles should become the
principles of school practice. As explained in previous chapters, the
psychological principles are represented in such practices as close
cooperation of parents and educators to support student learning;
clear, measurable learning goals; effective teaching methods; close
monitoring of learning progress; and appropriate correctives, reinforcement, and incentives.

Despite substantial increases in spending, little progress has been made in the last three decades to systematically implement such practices. The evidence described in this book suggests two broad solutions. Studies of new technologies show they can represent the psychological principles more fully and furnish instruction better adapted to individual learners. In most cases, they enable learners to learn as much as through conventional methods but more conveniently and in less time; and in some cases they are superior. Technologies, moreover, are rapidly improving and can be delivered whenever convenient to remote locations including schools and students' homes.

The second promising solution is parental choice of schools. Students in charter schools, parochial schools, and independent private schools exceed on average comparable students in public schools. But many middle-class and poor families live in areas without charter schools, and many parents cannot afford private school tuition. U.S. and foreign research supports the efficacy of vouchers to enable families to send their children to private schools of their own choosing, but few American families have been offered vouchers to enable them to choose their children's schools. Other countries made vouchers widely available, and extensive research shows their success.

Of the countries with nationwide vouchers, Sweden is the western country closest in income to the United States. Swedish research shows that nationwide vouchers yield excellent achievement results and parent satisfaction. Perhaps surprisingly, Swedish for-profit schools are growing the fastest and, with 30 campuses, the largest for-profit school firm exemplifies the efficient integration of technology and instructional practices that efficiently incorporates the psychological principles of learning.

ABOUT THE AUTHOR

Herbert J. Walberg is Distinguished Visiting Fellow at Stanford University's Hoover Institution and a project investigator at the Vanderbilt University National Center on School Choice. He formerly taught at Harvard University and is Emeritus University Scholar and Professor of Education and Psychology at the University of Illinois at Chicago.

Holding a Ph.D. from the University of Chicago, he wrote or edited more than 55 books and has written about 350 articles on such topics as educational effectiveness and exceptional human accomplishments. Among his latest books are the *International Encyclopedia of Educational Evaluation* and *Psychology and Educational Practice*. Since joining the Hoover Institution in 2000, he edited two books and written chapters in five other books on education policy.

Elected as a fellow of five academic organizations including the American Association for the Advancement of Science, American Psychological Association, and the Royal Statistical Society, Walberg is a founding fellow of the International Academy of Education, headquartered in Brussels. He edits for the Academy a booklet series on effective educational practices, which is distributed to some 4,000 educational leaders in more than 100 United Nations countries.

Walberg has given invited lectures to educators and policy makers in Australia, Belgium, China, England, France, Germany, Italy, Israel, Japan, the Netherlands South Africa, Sweden, Taiwan,

Venezuela, and the United States. He has frequently testified before U.S. Congressional committees, state legislators, and federal courts. He was a founding member of the National Assessment Governing Board, which sets policy for the National Assessment of Educational Progress (NAEP) and which was given the mission by Congress to measure the K–12 school achievement trends in the major school subjects.

In his research, Walberg employs experiments and analyses of large national and international data sets to discover the factors in homes, schools, and communities that promote learning and other human accomplishments. He also employs research synthesis to summarize effects of various educational conditions and methods on learning and other outcomes, the results of which have important bearings on education policy and practice.

For the U.S. Department of Education and the National Science Foundation, he carried out comparative research in Japanese and American schools. For the U.S. Department of State and the White House, he organized a radio broadcast series and book about American education, which is distributed in 74 countries. Walberg chaired the Scientific Advisory Group for the Paris-based Organization for Economic Cooperation and Development project on international education indicators and advised United Nations Educational Scientific, and Cultural Organization and government officials of Israel, Japan, Singapore, Sweden, and the U.K. on education research and policy. He has served on seven non-profit boards, and is a trustee of the California-based Foundation for Teaching Economics.

Walberg was appointed by the president and approved by the senate as a founding member of the National Board of Educational Sciences. The Board plans and oversees more than an annual $660 million on education research.

ABOUT THE HOOVER INSTITUTION'S
KORET TASK FORCE ON K–12 EDUCATION

The Koret Task Force on K–12 Education is a top-rate team of education experts brought together by the Hoover Institution at Stanford University, with the support of the Koret Foundation and other foundations and individuals, to work on education reform. The primary objectives of the task force are to gather, evaluate, and disseminate existing evidence in an analytical context, and identify reform measures that will enhance the quality and productivity of K–12 education.

The Koret Task Force on K–12 Education includes some of the most highly regarded and best known education scholars in the nation. Most are professors at leading universities and many have served in various executive and advisory roles for federal, state, and local governments. Their combined expertise represents over 300 years of research and study in the field of education. Current members of the task force are John E. Chubb, Williamson M. Evers, Chester E. Finn Jr., Eric A. Hanushek, Paul T. Hill, Caroline M. Hoxby, Tom Loveless, Terry M. Moe, Paul E. Peterson, and Herbert J. Walberg.

The ten-member task force forms the centerpiece of the Hoover Institution's Initiative on American Educational Institutions and Academic Performance. In addition to producing original research, analysis, and recommendations in a growing body of work on the most important issues in American education today, task force members serve as editors, contributors, and members of the editorial board of *Education Next: A Journal of Opinion and Research*, published by the Hoover Institution.

For further information, see the task force website:
www.hoover.org/taskforces/taskforces/education

INDEX

EDUCATION Next BOOKS address major subjects related to efforts to reform American public education. This imprint features assessments and monographs by Hoover Institution fellows (including members of the Hoover Institution's Koret Task Force on K–12 Education), as well as those of outside experts.